911100000014868

D1138665

Longman
Shakes

Much Ado About Nothing

itor: John O'Connor
xtual Consultant: Dr Stewart Eames

ume Editor: Kelly Newman

SE Assessment Practice:
ris Sutcliffe (AQA)
m Taylor (Edexcel)
rgaret Graham (WJEC)

Longman
Part of Pearson

Longman is an imprint of Pearson Education Limited, a company incorporated in England and Wales, having its registered office at Edinburgh Gate, Harlow, Essex, CM20 2JE. Registered company number: 872828

www.pearsonschoolsandfecolleges.co.uk

Longman is a registered trademark of Pearson Education Limited

© Pearson Education Limited 2010
The rights of Dr Stewart Eames, John O'Connor, Kelly Newman, Chris Sutcliffe, Pam Taylor and Margaret Graham to be identified as the authors of this work have been asserted by them in accordance with the Copyright, Designs and Patents Act 1988

First published 2004
This new edition published 2010

12 11 10
10 9 8 7 6 5 4 3 2 1

British Library Cataloguing in Publication Data
A catalogue record for this book is available from the British Library

ISBN 9781408236871

Copyright notice
All rights reserved. No part of this publication may be reproduced in any form or by any means (including photocopying or storing it in any medium by electronic means and whether or not transiently or incidentally to some other use of this publication) without the written permission of the copyright owner, except in accordance with the provisions of the Copyright, Designs and Patents Act 1988 or under the terms of a licence issued by the Copyright Licensing Agency, Saffron House, 6-10 Kirby Street, London EC1N 8TS (www.cla.co.uk). Applications for the copyright owner's written permission should be addressed to the publisher.

Typeset by Juice Creative Ltd, Hertfordshire
Cover photo © Corbis: Trinette Reed
Printed and bound in Great Britain by Henry Ling Limited, at the Dorset Press, Dorchester, DT1 1HD

We are grateful to the following for permission to reproduce copyright photographs:

Getty Image: *page 191*: Andrea Pistolesi/The Image Bank

Every effort has been made to contact copyright holders of material reproduced in this book. Any omissions will be rectified in subsequent printings if notice is given to the publishers.

BRENT LIBRARIES	
91110000014868	
Bertrams	21/06/2010
822.33	£4.99
BRKIN	

CONTENTS

ACT 1: SCENE BY SCENE

1 Don Pedro and his soldiers, who have just won a battle, arrive in Messina to stay with Leonato. As soon as they arrive, Benedick and Beatrice start quarrelling. Claudio tells Benedick that he is in love with Leonato's daughter, Hero. Don Pedro approves of this and offers to woo Hero for Claudio and to speak to Leonato on his behalf.

2 Antonio tells Leonato that he has heard that Don Pedro is in love with Hero and that he is going to propose to her that night. Leonato is amazed and delighted. He suggests that they should tell Hero and wait to see what happens.

3 After the battle, Don John has been forced to accept a reconciliation with his brother, Don Pedro, but he still wants to cause trouble. Conrade advises him to hide how he feels, but Don John says that he can't because being a villain is part of his nature. Borachio tells Don John that Claudio wants to marry Hero, and Don John immediately looks for a way that he can use this news to spoil Claudio's happiness.

ACT 2: SCENE BY SCENE

1 Leonato advises Hero to say yes if Don Pedro asks her to
marry him. During the masked ball, Don Pedro talks to Hero.
Don John maliciously tells Claudio that Don Pedro has won
Hero for himself – Claudio is devastated. Benedick also
thinks that he saw Don Pedro wooing Hero, but Don Pedro
convinces them that he was trying to win her for Claudio,
and the wedding is arranged. Beatrice has upset Benedick
by teasing him while they danced together, but Don Pedro
suggests that they would make a perfect couple. He asks the
others to help him make them fall in love with one another.

2 Borachio suggests another plan to spoil Claudio's happiness
and cause trouble: they could make Claudio believe that
Hero has been unfaithful to him. Don John is pleased by this
idea and promises to pay Borachio for helping him carry it
out.

3 Benedick complains about how Claudio has changed
since he fell in love. When he sees Don Pedro, Claudio
and Leonato, Benedick hides and overhears them loudly
discussing Beatrice's love for him which they have agreed to
do in order to trick him. Benedick believes them and, when
they have gone, he declares that he is in love with her too.

ACT 3: SCENE BY SCENE

1 To trick Beatrice, Hero and Ursula discuss Benedick's love for her, knowing that she is listening. She also hears them criticise her attitude towards men and marriage. Beatrice is upset that she seems so proud to others and decides to return Benedick's love.

2 Benedick is teased by Don Pedro, Claudio and Leonato about how his appearance and behaviour have changed. Don Pedro and Claudio are very happy that their plan to make him fall in love with Beatrice has been successful. Don John comes to tell them that Hero has been unfaithful to Claudio.

3 Dogberry and Verges give the watchmen their duties. The Watch overhear Borachio boast to Conrade that Don John has paid him well for his role in the plot to shame Hero. The watchmen leap from their hiding place and arrest Conrade and Borachio.

4 Margaret is helping Hero to prepare for her wedding when Beatrice arrives, claiming to have a head-cold. Margaret teases her for being love-sick over Benedick.

5 Dogberry and Verges tell Leonato that they have arrested Conrade and Borachio. However, their message is so garbled that when Leonato finally understands them, he does not have time to do anything himself. He is rushing to Hero's wedding, so tells them to question the prisoners themselves.

ACT 4: SCENE BY SCENE

1 At the wedding Claudio shames Hero by announcing that she is not a virgin. Don Pedro and Don John support this claim. Leonato believes them and is furious with Hero, who faints. Once the men have left, Friar Francis suggests that, to make Claudio feel regret, they pretend Hero has died. Beatrice and Benedick reveal their love for one another. Beatrice is furious with Claudio for shaming her cousin Hero, and persuades Benedick to challenge Claudio to a duel.

2 Conrade and Borachio are questioned by the Sexton and the watchmen reveal what they overheard about Don John's plot to shame Hero. The Sexton announces that Don John has run away and Hero has died.

ACT 5: SCENE BY SCENE

1 Antonio tries to comfort Leonato, who is devastated that Hero has been disgraced. They both challenge Claudio to a duel. Benedick enters and also challenges Claudio to a duel. Dogberry and Verges bring their prisoners, Conrade and Borachio, to Leonato. Borachio confesses his guilt. Claudio submits himself to Leonato, and Leonato commands him to marry Antonio's daughter.

2 Benedick tells Beatrice that he has challenged Claudio. They are then told by Ursula that Hero has been proved innocent and that Don John is the villain behind the plot.

3 Claudio mourns with Don Pedro at Hero's tomb. They leave to prepare for Claudio's wedding.

4 Before the second wedding, Benedick tells Leonato that he wants to marry Beatrice. Don Pedro and Claudio tease him. Hero, Beatrice, Margaret and Ursula enter, wearing masks. When Claudio says he will marry this 'new' wife, she takes off her mask, and is revealed to be Hero. Beatrice and Benedick publicly declare their love for each other. A messenger announces that Don John has been taken prisoner.

LEONATO'S HOUSEHOLD

LEONATO
Governor of Messina
He allows Hero to marry Claudio. After her shaming, he oversees a plan to ensure a happy ending.

ANTONIO
Leonato's older brother
He comforts Leonato after the shaming of Hero.

HERO
Leonato's only child
She is publicly shamed when she is falsely accused of being unfaithful to her fiancé, Claudio.

BEATRICE
Leonato's niece, an orphan
She constantly quarrels with Benedick, but later admits her love for him.

MARGARET
Hero's gentlewoman
She is involved, without realising it, in the plot to shame Hero.

URSULA
Hero's gentlewoman
She gossips with Hero to trick Beatrice into believing that Benedick is in love with her.

THE WATCH

DOGBERRY
Head Constable of the Watch
His mistakes and misunderstandings stop Don John's trick coming to light before the wedding.

VERGES
Dogberry's assistant
He tries to tell Leonato about the arrest of Conrade and Borachio.

MEN OF THE WATCH
Part-time police
They arrest Conrade and Borachio for the wrong offence, but help to uncover the plot to shame Hero.

OTHERS IN MESSINA

FRIAR FRANCIS
The priest at Hero and Claudio's wedding
He believes Hero is innocent and suggests they pretend she has died.

SEXTON
Church official who also takes down statements from prisoners
He sees the importance of Borachio's evidence and arranges to tell Leonato.

THE VISITING SOLDIERS

DON PEDRO
Prince of Aragon
He helps Claudio to win Hero
and he later supports Claudio
when he shames her.

CLAUDIO
Young officer under Don Pedro
He falls in love with Hero, but is
tricked into shaming her at their
wedding.

BENEDICK
Officer under Don Pedro
He claims he will never marry, but is
happy to discover that Beatrice loves
him.

BALTHASAR
Follower of Don Pedro
A singer

DON JOHN
Don Pedro's illegitimate brother
He remains angry with Don Pedro
and carries out the plot to trick
Claudio.

BORACHIO
Follower of Don John
He suggests to Don John the plot to
trick Claudio into shaming Hero.

CONRADE
Follower of Don John

LEONATO'S HOUSEHOLD

> LEONATO *Governor of Messina*
>
> ANTONIO *his brother, an old man*
>
> HERO *Leonato's daughter*
>
> MARGARET
> URSULA } *Hero's attendants*
>
> BEATRICE *Leonato's niece*
>
> A BOY
>
> ATTENDANTS

VISITORS

> DON PEDRO *Prince of Aragon*
>
> CLAUDIO *of Florence*
> BENEDICK *of Padua* } *lords, Don Pedro's companions*
>
> DON JOHN *Don Pedro's bastard half-brother*
>
> BORACHIO
> CONRADE } *Don John's followers*
>
> BALTHASAR *a singer*
>
> GENTLEMEN

OTHERS

> FRIAR FRANCIS *a priest*
>
> DOGBERRY *the Constable in charge of the Watch*
>
> VERGES *Dogberry's partner*
>
> A SEXTON
>
> MEN OF THE WATCH *part-time police*
>
> MUSICIANS
>
> MESSENGERS

The play is set in Messina, Italy.

In this scene ...

- Don Pedro arrives at the house of Leonato with his soldiers and his bastard brother Don John. It is announced that Claudio has proved himself to be a good soldier in the recent battle.
- Beatrice and Benedick resume their habit of quarrelling with each other.
- Claudio tells Benedick that he has fallen in love with Hero, Leonato's daughter.
- Don Pedro offers to win Hero's love for Claudio.

A messenger tells Leonato, the Governor of Messina, that Don Pedro and his soldiers are approaching.

3 **three leagues**: about nine miles

5 **action**: battle

6 **sort**: kind / rank
none of name: no-one of importance

10 **remembered**: rewarded
12 **in the figure of a lamb**: i.e. Claudio looks young
13 **bettered**: surpassed / exceeded

18–19 **joy ... bitterness**: he could not express his joy without weeping

THINK ABOUT for GCSE

22 **kind**: natural

Characterisation

- What are your impressions of Leonato from these opening moments?

Outside Leonato's house.

Enter LEONATO (*Governor of Messina*), *his daughter* HERO, *his niece* BEATRICE, *and a* MESSENGER.

LEONATO	I learn in this letter that Don Pedro of Aragon comes this night to Messina.
MESSENGER	He is very near by this; he was not three leagues off when I left him.
LEONATO	How many gentlemen have you lost in this action? 5
MESSENGER	But few of any sort, and none of name.
LEONATO	A victory is twice itself when the achiever brings home full numbers. I find here that Don Pedro hath bestowed much honour on a young Florentine called Claudio.
MESSENGER	Much deserved on his part and equally remembered by 10 Don Pedro. He hath borne himself beyond the promise of his age, doing in the figure of a lamb the feats of a lion. He hath indeed better bettered expectation than you must expect of me to tell you how.
LEONATO	He hath an uncle here in Messina will be very much 15 glad of it.
MESSENGER	I have already delivered him letters, and there appears much joy in him; even so much that joy could not show itself modest enough without a badge of bitterness.
LEONATO	Did he break out into tears? 20
MESSENGER	In great measure.
LEONATO	A kind overflow of kindness. There are no faces truer than those that are so washed. How much better is it to weep at joy than to joy at weeping!
BEATRICE	I pray you, is Signior Mountanto returned from the wars, 25 or no?

Leonato's niece Beatrice asks mockingly about Benedick, one of Don Pedro's soldiers.

31 **pleasant**: entertaining

32–3 **He set up … flight**: He posted advertisements challenging the god of love to defeat him, i.e. Benedick used to boast that he would never fall in love.

34 **subscribed for**: accepted the challenge on behalf of

34–5 **at the bird-bolt**: to a contest with blunt arrows

38 **tax**: criticise

39 **be meet**: get even

41 **musty victual**: stale food
holp: helped

42 **valiant trencher-man**: hearty eater

43 **stomach**: appetite

45 **to**: in comparison with

48 **stuffed man**: i.e. a tailor's dummy, stuffed to look like a man

THINK ABOUT *for* GCSE

Relationships

- How do you think Beatrice feels about Benedick?
- How far do you believe Beatrice's criticisms of Benedick?

Language

- What do you notice about the language used in lines 50 to 54 to describe their relationship?

54 **five wits**: i.e. brain power
halting: limping

54–8 **and now … creature**: i.e. Beatrice got the better of Benedick's wit; she says that he is now barely more intelligent than his horse.

MESSENGER	I know none of that name, lady; there was none such in the army of any sort.
LEONATO	What is he that you ask for, niece?
HERO	My cousin means Signior Benedick of Padua. 30
MESSENGER	O, he's returned, and as pleasant as ever he was.
BEATRICE	He set up his bills here in Messina, and challenged Cupid at the flight; and my uncle's fool, reading the challenge, subscribed for Cupid, and challenged him at the bird-bolt. I pray you, how many hath he killed and 35 eaten in these wars? But how many hath he killed? For indeed I promised to eat all of his killing.
LEONATO	Faith, niece, you tax Signior Benedick too much; but he'll be meet with you, I doubt it not.
MESSENGER	He hath done good service, lady, in these wars. 40
BEATRICE	You had musty victual, and he hath holp to eat it. He is a very valiant trencher-man; he hath an excellent stomach.
MESSENGER	And a good soldier too, lady.
BEATRICE	And a good soldier to a lady. But what is he to a lord? 45
MESSENGER	A lord to a lord, a man to a man, stuffed with all honourable virtues.
BEATRICE	It is so, indeed; he is no less than a stuffed man. But for the stuffing – well, we are all mortal.
LEONATO	You must not, sir, mistake my niece. There is a kind 50 of merry war betwixt Signior Benedick and her. They never meet but there's a skirmish of wit between them.
BEATRICE	Alas, he gets nothing by that. In our last conflict four of his five wits went halting off, and now is the whole man governed with one: so that if he have wit enough 55 to keep himself warm, let him bear it for a difference between himself and his horse; for it is all the wealth that he hath left, to be known a reasonable creature. Who is his companion now? He hath every month a new sworn brother. 60

Don Pedro enters and is greeted warmly by Leonato.

62 faith: loyalty

63 it … block: it changes with every new fashion

64 books: good books

65 an: if

66 squarer: brawler

70 pestilence: plague

71 presently: immediately

73 ere 'a be: before he is

81 encounter it: seek it out

86 embrace your charge: welcome your trouble / expense

THINK ABOUT *for* **GCSE**

Characterisation

- What are your impressions of Beatrice so far? Think about the way she uses language and how she responds to the messenger.

MESSENGER	Is't possible?
BEATRICE	Very easily possible. He wears his faith but as the fashion of his hat: it ever changes with the next block.
MESSENGER	I see, lady, the gentleman is not in your books.
BEATRICE	No: an he were, I would burn my study. But, I pray you, who is his companion? Is there no young squarer now that will make a voyage with him to the devil? 65
MESSENGER	He is most in the company of the right noble Claudio.
BEATRICE	O Lord, he will hang upon him like a disease. He is sooner caught than the pestilence, and the taker runs presently mad. God help the noble Claudio! If he have caught the Benedick, it will cost him a thousand pound ere 'a be cured. 70
MESSENGER	I will hold friends with you, lady.
BEATRICE	Do, good friend. 75
LEONATO	*You* will never run mad, niece.
BEATRICE	No, not till a hot January.
MESSENGER	Don Pedro is approached.

Enter DON PEDRO, CLAUDIO, BENEDICK, BALTHASAR, *and* DON JOHN *the bastard (Don Pedro's half-brother)*.

DON PEDRO	Good Signior Leonato, are you come to meet your trouble? The fashion of the world is to avoid cost, and you encounter it. 80
LEONATO	Never came trouble to my house in the likeness of your Grace. For trouble being gone, comfort should remain; but when you depart from me sorrow abides, and happiness takes his leave. 85
DON PEDRO	You embrace your charge too willingly. (*Indicating* HERO) I think this is your daughter.
LEONATO	Her mother hath many times told me so.
BENEDICK	Were you in doubt, sir, that you asked her?
LEONATO	Signior Benedick, no; for then were you a child. 90

15

When Don Pedro and Leonato move away, Beatrice and Benedick immediately begin quarrelling.

91 **have it full**: are well answered
92 **fathers herself**: looks like her father

95-7 **If ... she is**: i.e. Hero would not want Leonato's head on her shoulders as he is old and grey.

99 **marks**: listens to

102 **meet**: ideal

104 **turncoat**: i.e. something that changes sides

108 **dear happiness**: great stroke of luck
109 **pernicious**: extremely harmful
110 **humour for that**: frame of mind in that respect

114 **predestinate**: inevitable

118 **rare parrot-teacher**: excellent repeater of empty words

120-1 **so good a continuer**: had such stamina

THINK ABOUT
for GCSE

Characterisation

• Does Beatrice or Benedick come out better from their quarrel? How?

DON PEDRO	You have it full, Benedick: we may guess by this what you are, being a man. Truly, the lady fathers herself. (*To* HERO) Be happy, lady; for you are like an honourable father.
BENEDICK	If Signior Leonato be her father, she would not have 95 his head on her shoulders for all Messina, as like him as she is.

DON PEDRO *and* LEONATO *move aside to talk.*

BEATRICE	I wonder that you will still be talking, Signior Benedick. Nobody marks you.
BENEDICK	What, my dear Lady Disdain! Are you yet living? 100
BEATRICE	Is it possible disdain should die while she hath such meet food to feed it as Signior Benedick? Courtesy itself must convert to disdain, if you come in her presence.
BENEDICK	Then is courtesy a turncoat. But it is certain I am loved of all ladies, only you excepted; and I would I could 105 find in my heart that I had not a hard heart, for, truly, I love none.
BEATRICE	A dear happiness to women: they would else have been troubled with a pernicious suitor! I thank God and my cold blood, I am of your humour for that. I had rather 110 hear my dog bark at a crow than a man swear he loves me.
BENEDICK	God keep your ladyship still in that mind! So some gentleman or other shall 'scape a predestinate scratched face. 115
BEATRICE	Scratching could not make it worse, an 'twere such a face as yours were.
BENEDICK	Well, you are a rare parrot-teacher.
BEATRICE	A bird of my tongue is better than a beast of yours.
BENEDICK	I would my horse had the speed of your tongue, and so 120 good a continuer. But keep your way, a' God's name. I have done.

While the others go into Leonato's house, Claudio and Benedick remain behind. Claudio has fallen in love with Leonato's daughter Hero.

123 a jade's trick: A jade is a badly trained horse; the trick may be that the horse slips out of its harness.

130 be forsworn: have to break your word

139 noted her not: took no special notice of her
140 modest: sweet / shy

143 after my custom: in the way I usually do
professed: self-proclaimed
tyrant: i.e. critic

146 low: short
147 brown: dark-complexioned

THINK ABOUT for GCSE

Relationships

- Beatrice says about Benedick, 'I know you of old' (line 123). What does this suggest about her previous relationship with him?

Themes and issues

- **Men and women**: What do we learn in this scene about his attitude towards women?

Characterisation

- What do we know about Don John so far?

Beatrice	You always end with a jade's trick: I know you of old.
Don Pedro	... That is the sum of all, Leonato. Signior Claudio and Signior Benedick, my dear friend Leonato hath invited 125 you all. I tell him we shall stay here at the least a month, and he heartily prays some occasion may detain us longer. I dare swear he is no hypocrite, but prays from his heart.
Leonato	If you swear, my lord, you shall not be forsworn. 130 (*To* Don John) Let me bid you welcome, my lord, being reconciled to the Prince your brother. I owe you all duty.
Don John	I thank you. I am not of many words, but I thank you.
Leonato	Please it your Grace lead on? 135
Don Pedro	Your hand, Leonato: we will go together.

All exit except Benedick *and* Claudio.

Claudio	Benedick, didst thou note the daughter of Signior Leonato?
Benedick	I noted her not, but I looked on her.
Claudio	Is she not a modest young lady? 140
Benedick	Do you question me as an honest man should do, for my simple true judgement? Or would you have me speak after my custom, as being a professed tyrant to their sex?
Claudio	No, I pray thee speak in sober judgement. 145
Benedick	Why, i'faith, methinks she's too low for a high praise, too brown for a fair praise, and too little for a great praise. Only this commendation I can afford her, that were she other than she is, she were unhandsome; and being no other but as she is, I do not like her. 150
Claudio	Thou thinkest I am in sport. I pray thee tell me truly how thou likest her.
Benedick	Would you buy her, that you inquire after her?
Claudio	Can the world buy such a jewel?

Benedick laughs at Claudio for suddenly falling in love with Hero and tells Don Pedro all about it.

156 **sad**: serious
flouting Jack: mocking rascal
157–8 **Cupid … carpenter**: i.e. tell outrageous lies (Proverb and legend said that Cupid was blind and Vulcan was a blacksmith.)
159 **go in the song**: fit in with your mood

169 **but … suspicion**: who does not want to get married (Refers to the Elizabethan joke that the husband of an unfaithful wife grew horns.)
170 **Go to**: Come, come!
170–1 **an thou wilt needs**: if you must
172 **sigh away Sundays**: spend Sundays at home with your wife

176 **constrain**: compel

181 **your Grace's part**: the question you are supposed to ask
183 **If … uttered**: i.e. If I had said this, that's how Benedick would have reported it

THINK ABOUT for GCSE

Characterisation

• What does Benedick reveal about himself in his responses to Claudio (from line 137 to 173)?

BENEDICK   Yea, and a case to put it into. But speak you this with   155
a sad brow? Or do you play the flouting Jack, to tell
us Cupid is a good hare-finder, and Vulcan a rare
carpenter? Come, in what key shall a man take you to
go in the song?

CLAUDIO   In mine eye she is the sweetest lady that ever I looked on.   160

BENEDICK   I can see yet without spectacles, and I see no such
matter. There's her cousin, an she were not possessed
with a fury, exceeds her as much in beauty as the first
of May doth the last of December. But I hope you have
no intent to turn husband, have you?   165

CLAUDIO   I would scarce trust myself, though I had sworn the
contrary, if Hero would be my wife.

BENEDICK   Is't come to this? In faith, hath not the world one man
but he will wear his cap with suspicion? Shall I never
see a bachelor of threescore again? Go to, i'faith; an   170
thou wilt needs thrust thy neck into a yoke, wear the
print of it, and sigh away Sundays. Look, Don Pedro is
returned to seek you.

Enter DON PEDRO.

DON PEDRO   What secret hath held you here, that you followed not
to Leonato's?   175

BENEDICK   I would your Grace would constrain me to tell.

DON PEDRO   I charge thee on thy allegiance.

BENEDICK   You hear, Count Claudio. I can be secret as a dumb
man. I would have you think so; but, on my allegiance,
mark you this, on my allegiance – he is in love. With   180
who? Now that is your Grace's part. Mark how short his
answer is: with Hero, Leonato's short daughter.

CLAUDIO   If this were so, so were it uttered.

BENEDICK   Like the old tale, my lord: 'It is not so, nor 'twas not so;
but indeed, God forbid it should be so!'   185

CLAUDIO   If my passion change not shortly, God forbid it should
be otherwise!

Don Pedro and Claudio side with each other against Benedick's negative view of love and marriage.

189 **fetch me in**: trick me

190 **troth**: faith / truth

198 **heretic**: unbeliever
     despite of: contempt for

200–1 **maintain ... will**: keep up his pose of being a woman-hater except by sheer will-power

204 **recheat**: call on a hunting horn
205 **baldrick**: A belt worn over the shoulder for holding a bugle.
206 **shall pardon me**: must excuse me
208 **fine**: conclusion

THINK ABOUT for GCSE

Context

- There are many references in plays of the Early Modern era to 'cuckolds' (men whose wives were unfaithful) and the idea that a cuckold grew horns that everyone but him could see. How does Benedick reveal his own fear of cuckoldry here?

212 **lose more blood**: Elizabethans believed that love-sick sighs drained blood from the heart but wine would restore it.
214 **ballad-maker**: one who writes love songs
215 **for ... Cupid**: as a brothel sign

217 **notable argument**: outstanding subject for discussion
218 **bottle**: A wicker basket, here, used for target practice.
220 **Adam**: a famous archer

DON PEDRO	Amen, if you love her; for the lady is very well worthy.
CLAUDIO	You speak this to fetch me in, my lord.
DON PEDRO	By my troth, I speak my thought. 190
CLAUDIO	And in faith, my lord, I spoke mine.
BENEDICK	And by my two faiths and troths, my lord, I spoke mine.
CLAUDIO	That I love her, I feel.
DON PEDRO	That she is worthy, I know.
BENEDICK	That I neither feel how she should be loved, nor know 195 how she should be worthy, is the opinion that fire cannot melt out of me. I will die in it at the stake.
DON PEDRO	Thou wast ever an obstinate heretic in the despite of beauty.
CLAUDIO	And never could maintain his part but in the force of his 200 will.
BENEDICK	That a woman conceived me, I thank her: that she brought me up, I likewise give her most humble thanks. But that I will have a recheat winded in my forehead, or hang my bugle in an invisible baldrick, all women 205 shall pardon me. Because I will not do them the wrong to mistrust any, I will do myself the right to trust none: and the fine is, for the which I may go the finer, I will live a bachelor.
DON PEDRO	I shall see thee, ere I die, look pale with love. 210
BENEDICK	With anger, with sickness, or with hunger, my lord, not with love. Prove that ever I lose more blood with love than I will get again with drinking, pick out mine eyes with a ballad-maker's pen, and hang me up at the door of a brothel-house for the sign of blind Cupid. 215
DON PEDRO	Well, if ever thou dost fall from this faith, thou wilt prove a notable argument.
BENEDICK	If I do, hang me in a bottle like a cat, and shoot at me; and he that hits me, let him be clapped on the shoulder, and called Adam. 220

Don Pedro asks Benedick to go and tell Leonato that he will return for dinner. Claudio asks Don Pedro for his support in winning Hero.

THINK ABOUT *for* GCSE

Language

• What is Don Pedro suggesting about Benedick in his animal image (lines 221 to 222)?

• At line 245 there is a change from prose to verse/poetry. What is the effect of this?

Context

• A young man like Claudio would take a great interest in how much money a bride might bring to the marriage. Does his question to Don Pedro (line 249) make him seem like a fortune-hunter, in your opinion?

221 **as time shall try**: time will tell
221–2 **'In time ... yoke'**: i.e. even the wildest beast can be tamed

229 **horn-mad**: stark mad (with an obvious reference to the cuckold's horns)

230 **spent all his quiver**: used up all his arrows, i.e. done all his work
Venice: A city noted for sexual immorality.

233 **temporize with the hours**: change your ways over time

237 **matter**: substance
238 **embassage**: mission / task
and so I commit you: a conventional form of closing letters

242 **guarded with fragments**: decorated with scraps
242–3 **the guards ... basted on**: i.e. the decorative words have little connection to the point
243 **flout old ends**: mock conventional phrases

247 **apt**: quick

251 **affect**: love

Don Pedro	Well, as time shall try: 'In time the savage bull doth bear the yoke.'
Benedick	The savage bull may: but if ever the sensible Benedick bear it, pluck off the bull's horns and set them in my forehead, and let me be vilely painted – and, in such 225 great letters as they write 'Here is good horse to hire', let them signify under my sign 'Here you may see Benedick, the married man.'
Claudio	If this should ever happen, thou wouldst be horn-mad.
Don Pedro	Nay, if Cupid have not spent all his quiver in Venice, 230 thou wilt quake for this shortly.
Benedick	I look for an earthquake too, then.
Don Pedro	Well, you will temporize with the hours. In the meantime, good Signior Benedick, repair to Leonato's, commend me to him, and tell him I will not fail him at 235 supper; for indeed he hath made great preparation.
Benedick	I have almost matter enough in me for such an embassage; and so I commit you –
Claudio	To the tuition of God. From my house, if I had it –
Don Pedro	The sixth of July. Your loving friend, Benedick. 240
Benedick	Nay, mock not, mock not. The body of your discourse is sometime guarded with fragments, and the guards are but slightly basted on neither. Ere you flout old ends any further, examine your conscience: and so I leave you.

Exit.

Claudio	My liege, your Highness now may do me good. 245
Don Pedro	My love is thine to teach. Teach it but how, And thou shalt see how apt it is to learn Any hard lesson that may do thee good.
Claudio	Hath Leonato any son, my lord?
Don Pedro	No child but Hero: she's his only heir. 250 Dost thou affect her, Claudio?

Don Pedro approves the match. He offers to win Hero for Claudio and to talk to Leonato about it.

252 **ended action**: recent battle

264 **break with**: broach the subject to

268 **complexion**: appearance
270 **salved**: softened
treatise: discussion
272 **The fairest ... necessity**: The best gift is the one that fulfils the need.
273 **Look what**: Whatever
'Tis ... lovest: 1 in short you're in love; 2 you fall in love only once
274 **fit thee**: provide you

THINK ABOUT for GCSE

Context

• Why might Don Pedro have offered to win Hero for Claudio? What does it tell us about courtship conventions in Early Modern times?

Relationships

• How would you describe the relationship between Don Pedro and Claudio?

CLAUDIO	O my lord,
	When you went onward on this ended action,
	I looked upon her with a soldier's eye,
	That liked, but had a rougher task in hand
	Than to drive liking to the name of love. 255
	But now I am returned, and that war-thoughts
	Have left their places vacant, in their rooms
	Come thronging soft and delicate desires,
	All prompting me how fair young Hero is,
	Saying I liked her ere I went to wars. 260

CLAUDIO

                        O my lord,
When you went onward on this ended action,
I looked upon her with a soldier's eye,
That liked, but had a rougher task in hand
Than to drive liking to the name of love.   255
But now I am returned, and that war-thoughts
Have left their places vacant, in their rooms
Come thronging soft and delicate desires,
All prompting me how fair young Hero is,
Saying I liked her ere I went to wars.   260

DON PEDRO

Thou wilt be like a lover presently,
And tire the hearer with a book of words.
If thou dost love fair Hero, cherish it;
And I will break with her and with her father
And thou shalt have her. Was't not to this end   265
That thou began'st to twist so fine a story?

CLAUDIO

How sweetly you do minister to love,
That know love's grief by his complexion!
But lest my liking might too sudden seem,
I would have salved it with a longer treatise.   270

DON PEDRO

What need the bridge much broader than the flood?
The fairest grant is the necessity.
Look what will serve is fit. 'Tis once, thou lovest,
And I will fit thee with the remedy.
I know we shall have revelling tonight: 275
I will assume thy part in some disguise,
And tell fair Hero I am Claudio,
And in her bosom I'll unclasp my heart,
And take her hearing prisoner with the force
And strong encounter of my amorous tale.   280
Then after, to her father will I break:
And the conclusion is, she shall be thine.
In practice let us put it presently.

Exeunt.

In this scene ...

- Leonato's brother Antonio hurries in with a false report: his servant has told him that Don Pedro is in love with Hero.
- Leonato is pleased to hear this but suggests that they wait to see what happens instead of questioning the servant more.

1   **cousin**: kinsman

6   **As ... them**: The outcome will determine if the news is good
7   **Prince**: i.e. Don Pedro
8   **thick-pleached**: closely-intertwined branches / heavily shaded
10 **discovered**: revealed
12 **accordant**: in agreement
13 **take ... top**: seize the moment
13–14 **break ... it**: broach the subject with you

15 **wit**: intelligence

18 **appear itself**: actually happens
19 **withal**: with it
20 **peradventure**: perhaps

23 **cry you mercy**: beg your pardon

THINK ABOUT for GCSE

Themes and issues

- This brief scene introduces the theme of **noting** (observing) **and misunderstanding**. How has Leonato come to believe that Don Pedro is in love with Hero? How far do you think wishful thinking is involved here?

Outside Leonato's house.

Enter LEONATO, *meeting an old man, his brother,* ANTONIO.

LEONATO	How now, brother! Where is my cousin, your son? Hath he provided this music?
ANTONIO	He is very busy about it. But, brother, I can tell you strange news that you yet dreamt not of.
LEONATO	Are they good? 5
ANTONIO	As the event stamps them; but they have a good cover, they show well outward. The Prince and Count Claudio, walking in a thick-pleached alley in mine orchard, were thus much overheard by a man of mine: the Prince discovered to Claudio that he loved my niece 10 your daughter, and meant to acknowledge it this night in a dance; and if he found her accordant, he meant to take the present time by the top and instantly break with you of it.
LEONATO	Hath the fellow any wit that told you this? 15
ANTONIO	A good sharp fellow. I will send for him, and question him yourself.
LEONATO	No, no. We will hold it as a dream till it appear itself. But I will acquaint my daughter withal, that she may be the better prepared for an answer, if peradventure this 20 be true. Go you and tell her of it.

Attendants cross the stage, led by Antonio's son, and accompanied by BALTHASAR *the musician.*

(*To Antonio's son*) Cousin, you know what you have to do. (*To the musician*) O, I cry you mercy, friend: go you with me, and I will use your skill. (*To Antonio's son*) Good cousin, have a care this busy time.   25

Exeunt.

In this scene ...

- Don John talks to Conrade about how unhappy he is about the current reconciliation with his brother, Don Pedro.
- Borachio enters with news of Claudio's intended marriage to Hero.
- Don John immediately starts to think of ways to destroy Claudio's happiness.

In the recent battle Don Pedro's opponent was his half-brother Don John. Now they are reconciled and Don John's companion Conrade advises him to hide his bitterness towards his brother.

1 **What the good-year**: What the devil
1–2 **out of measure**: excessively
3 **breeds**: causes it

7 **sufferance**: endurance
8–9 **born under Saturn**: i.e. of a gloomy or depressed personality
10 **mortifying mischief**: fatal disease

13 **tend on**: attend to
14 **claw**: flatter / accommodate
humour: mood
16–17 **stood out**: rebelled

18 **grace**: favour

21 **canker**: wild rose

23 **fashion a carriage**: put on a front

26 **enfranchized**: set free
clog: Heavy block of wood used to tether an animal.

THINK ABOUT for GCSE

Context

- Illegitimate sons were often denied any share of their father's titles or property and so became resentful. This might be one underlying reason for Don John's 'sadness' (line 4). What other reasons might he have? Look back at Act 1 Scene 1, lines 131 to 134.

Outside Leonato's house.

Enter DON JOHN *the bastard and* CONRADE *his companion.*

CONRADE	What the good-year, my lord! Why are you thus out of measure sad?
DON JOHN	There is no measure in the occasion that breeds; therefore the sadness is without limit.
CONRADE	You should hear reason. 5
DON JOHN	And when I have heard it, what blessing brings it?
CONRADE	If not a present remedy, at least a patient sufferance.
DON JOHN	I wonder that thou – being, as thou sayest thou art, born under Saturn – goest about to apply a moral medicine to a mortifying mischief. I cannot hide what I am. I must be 10 sad when I have cause, and smile at no man's jests; eat when I have stomach, and wait for no man's leisure; sleep when I am drowsy, and tend on no man's business; laugh when I am merry, and claw no man in his humour.
CONRADE	Yea, but you must not make the full show of this till you 15 may do it without controlment. You have of late stood out against your brother; and he hath ta'en you newly into his grace, where it is impossible you should take true root but by the fair weather that you make yourself. It is needful that you frame the season for your own harvest. 20
DON JOHN	I had rather be a canker in a hedge than a rose in his grace; and it better fits my blood to be disdained of all than to fashion a carriage to rob love from any. In this, though I cannot be said to be a flattering honest man, it must not be denied but I am a plain-dealing villain. I 25 am trusted with a muzzle and enfranchized with a clog: therefore I have decreed not to sing in my cage. If I had my mouth, I would bite; if I had my liberty, I would do my liking. In the meantime, let me be that I am, and seek not to alter me. 30
CONRADE	Can you make no use of your discontent?

Don John's other companion Borachio enters and tells them that Claudio is intending to marry Hero. Don John holds a grudge against Claudio because of the recent battle.

THINK ABOUT for GCSE

Characterisation

- Look at Don John's expressions of contempt for Claudio in lines 40 and 42. Why might he want to destroy Claudio's happiness? Think of two reasons.
- How would you describe Don John's personality from his appearance in this scene and Act 1 Scene 1?

38 **betroths ... unquietness**: engages himself to noise (which is inevitable in marriage)
39 **Marry**: by the Virgin Mary

42 **proper squire**: handsome fellow (used scornfully here)

45 **forward**: precocious
   March-chick: A chick which has hatched prematurely.
46 **entertained for**: hired as
   smoking: i.e. airing the room by burning something strong-smelling

49 **arras**: tapestry wall-hanging

53 **start-up**: upstart
54 **cross**: obstruct
55 **sure**: loyal

58 **were ... mind**: thought like me (i.e. and would poison their food)
59 **prove**: see / discover

DON JOHN   I make all use of it, for I use it only. Who comes here?

Enter BORACHIO.

What news, Borachio?

BORACHIO   I came yonder from a great supper. The Prince your brother is royally entertained by Leonato; and I can give **35** you intelligence of an intended marriage.

DON JOHN   Will it serve for any model to build mischief on? What is he for a fool that betroths himself to unquietness?

BORACHIO   Marry, it is your brother's right hand.

DON JOHN   Who? The most exquisite Claudio? **40**

BORACHIO   Even he.

DON JOHN   A proper squire! And who, and who? Which way looks he?

BORACHIO   Marry, on Hero, the daughter and heir of Leonato.

DON JOHN   A very forward March-chick! How came you to this? **45**

BORACHIO   Being entertained for a perfumer, as I was smoking a musty room, comes me the Prince and Claudio, hand in hand, in sad conference. I whipped me behind the arras, and there heard it agreed upon that the Prince should woo Hero for himself, and having obtained her, **50** give her to Count Claudio.

DON JOHN   Come, come, let us thither. This may prove food to my displeasure. That young start-up hath all the glory of my overthrow. If I can cross him any way, I bless myself every way. You are both sure, and will assist me? **55**

CONRADE   To the death, my lord.

DON JOHN   Let us to the great supper. Their cheer is the greater that I am subdued. Would the cook were o' my mind! Shall we go prove what's to be done?

BORACHIO   We'll wait upon your lordship. **60**

Exeunt.

In this scene ...

- Leonato advises his daughter on how to respond to a proposal from Don Pedro.
- The men enter for a masquerade dance.
- Don John tries to spoil things between Claudio and Hero, telling him that Don Pedro has won Hero for himself.
- Don Pedro explains that this is untrue. He has arranged with Leonato for Hero to marry Claudio.
- Don Pedro plans how to bring Beatrice and Benedick together.

Beatrice says that she is happy to be single but keeps mentioning Benedick and marriage in her conversation.

3   **tartly**: sourly

8   **image**: picture / statue
8–9   **my ... son**: a spoiled child

15   **'a**: he

17   **shrewd**: sharp

18   **curst**: bad-tempered

19–21   **Too curst ... none**: i.e. there will be one less cuckold if I don't get a husband (Refers to the Elizabethan joke that the husband of an unfaithful wife grew horns.)

23   **Just**: Exactly
24   **at Him**: praying to God

26   **the woollen**: rough woollen blankets

THINK ABOUT
for **GCSE**

Characterisation

- What is there in Beatrice's conversation that gives away how she really feels about Benedick?

34

Inside Leonato's house.

Enter LEONATO, ANTONIO, HERO, BEATRICE, MARGARET *and* URSULA.

LEONATO	Was not Count John here at supper?
ANTONIO	I saw him not.
BEATRICE	How tartly that gentleman looks! I never can see him but I am heart-burned an hour after.
HERO	He is of a very melancholy disposition. 5
BEATRICE	He were an excellent man that were made just in the midway between him and Benedick: the one is too like an image and says nothing, and the other too like my lady's eldest son, evermore tattling.
LEONATO	Then half Signior Benedick's tongue in Count John's 10 mouth, and half Count John's melancholy in Signior Benedick's face –
BEATRICE	With a good leg and a good foot, uncle, and money enough in his purse, such a man would win any woman in the world, if 'a could get her good will. 15
LEONATO	By my troth, niece, thou wilt never get thee a husband if thou be so shrewd of thy tongue.
ANTONIO	In faith, she's too curst.
BEATRICE	Too curst is more than curst. I shall lessen God's sending that way: for it is said, 'God sends a curst cow 20 short horns', but to a cow too curst he sends none.
LEONATO	So, by being too curst, God will send you no horns.
BEATRICE	Just, if he send me no husband – for the which blessing I am at Him upon my knees every morning and evening. Lord, I could not endure a husband with a beard on his 25 face! I had rather lie in the woollen.
LEONATO	You may light on a husband that hath no beard.

Beatrice continues to claim that she will never get married. She advises Hero to marry someone that she likes, not just someone who will please her father.

33 **even**: simply
    in earnest: in advance payment
34 **bear-ward**: bear-trainer
    lead ... hell: According to proverb, this was the fate of unmarried women.

41 **bachelors**: This term also applied to women.

THINK ABOUT for GCSE

Context

• There are a number of Shakespeare's plays that show the power that fathers had over their daughters in deciding whom they should marry. What view does Beatrice express in lines 45 to 48 about Hero's 'duty'?

Language

• Two statements are made to Hero (in lines 43 to 44 and 57 to 59) but she offers no reply. What do the two statements have in common?

Characterisation

• What does Hero's silence suggest about her?

51 **metal**: substance

54 **marl**: clay
54–5 **Adam's sons**: i.e. all men
55–6 **match ... kindred**: marry a close relative

58 **in that kind**: i.e. propose marriage

BEATRICE	What should I do with him? Dress him in my apparel and make him my waiting-gentlewoman? He that hath a beard is more than a youth, and he that hath no beard **30** is less than a man; and he that is more than a youth is not for me, and he that is less than a man, I am not for him. Therefore I will even take sixpence in earnest of the bear-ward, and lead his apes into hell.
LEONATO	Well then, go you into hell? **35**
BEATRICE	No, but to the gate – and there will the devil meet me, like an old cuckold with horns on his head, and say, 'Get you to heaven, Beatrice, get you to heaven: here's no place for you maids.' So deliver I up my apes and away to Saint Peter for the heavens. He shows me **40** where the bachelors sit, and there live we as merry as the day is long.
ANTONIO	(*To* HERO) Well, niece, I trust you will be ruled by your father.
BEATRICE	Yes, faith: it is my cousin's duty to make curtsey and **45** say, 'Father, as it please you'. But yet for all that, cousin, let him be a handsome fellow – or else make another curtsey and say, 'Father, as it please *me*'.
LEONATO	Well, niece, I hope to see *you* one day fitted with a husband. **50**
BEATRICE	Not till God make men of some other metal than earth. Would it not grieve a woman to be over-mastered with a piece of valiant dust? To make an account of her life to a clod of wayward marl? No, uncle, I'll none. Adam's sons are my brethren, and, truly, I hold it a sin to match **55** in my kindred.
LEONATO	(*To* HERO) Daughter, remember what I told you. If the Prince do solicit you in that kind, you know your answer.

Leonato's family believe that Don Pedro is going to try to win Hero. All the men enter in masks for the dance. Don Pedro begins to charm Hero.

61 **in good time**: 1 soon; 2 in time with the music (i.e. properly)
important: pushy
62 **measure**: 1 moderation; 2 a stately dance
64 **cinquepace**: lively dance

67 **state and ancientry**: stately tradition

70 **Cousin**: An all-purpose term for relative.
passing: more than / very

73 **walk a bout**: walk a while / dance
74 **So**: If

THINK ABOUT for GCSE

Themes and issues

• **Love, courtship and marriage**: What views does Beatrice express about marriage in lines 60 to 69?

Characterisation

• What does Hero's conversation with Don Pedro reveal about her?

79 **favour**: face
defend: forbid
80 **case**: i.e. his mask
81 **visor**: mask
Philemon ... Jove: Philemon, a peasant in a thatched cottage, welcomed Jove, the king of the gods, unaware of his identity.

| BEATRICE | The fault will be in the music, cousin, if you be not wooed | 60 |

BEATRICE   The fault will be in the music, cousin, if you be not wooed   60
in good time. If the Prince be too important, tell him there
is measure in everything and so dance out the answer.
For hear me, Hero: wooing, wedding, and repenting is as
a Scotch jig, a measure, and a cinquepace. The first suit
is hot and hasty, like a Scotch jig, and full as fantastical;   65
the wedding, mannerly-modest, as a measure, full of
state and ancientry; and then comes repentance and,
with his bad legs, falls into the cinquepace faster and
faster, till he sink into his grave.

LEONATO   Cousin, you apprehend passing shrewdly.   70

BEATRICE   I have a good eye, uncle. I can see a church by daylight.

LEONATO   The revellers are entering, brother. Make good room.

ANTONIO *and* LEONATO *put on their masks.*

Enter DON PEDRO, CLAUDIO, BENEDICK, BALTHASAR, DON JOHN,
BORACHIO *and others, in masks, with a drum. A slow dance*
begins.

DON PEDRO   Lady, will you walk a bout with your friend?

HERO   So you walk softly, and look sweetly, and say nothing,
I am yours for the walk; and especially when I walk away.   75

DON PEDRO   With me in your company?

HERO   I may say so, when I please.

DON PEDRO   And when please you to say so?

HERO   When I like your favour – for God defend the lute
should be like the case!   80

DON PEDRO   My visor is Philemon's roof: within the house is Jove.

HERO   Why then your visor should be thatched.

DON PEDRO   Speak low, if you speak love.

They move aside in the dance.

BALTHASAR   Well, I would you did like me.

MARGARET   So would not I, for your own sake. For I have many ill   85
qualities.

39

Some of the men playfully pretend that they are not who they are. Whilst dancing with Benedick, Beatrice is irritated by the things her dancing partner says to her.

93 **clerk**: Church official who leads the responses during services.

98 **counterfeit**: imitate

100 **dry hand**: a sign of old age
up and down: exactly

104 **mum**: silence

THINK ABOUT for GCSE

Performance and staging

• This scene involves not only speech, but music and dance. If you were directing it, how would you ensure that each pair of actors could be heard while the dance was carrying on?

111 **Hundred Merry Tales**: a joke book

BALTHASAR	Which is one?
MARGARET	I say my prayers aloud.
BALTHASAR	I love you the better: the hearers may cry 'Amen'.
MARGARET	God match me with a good dancer! 90
BALTHASAR	Amen.
MARGARET	And God keep him out of my sight when the dance is done! Answer, clerk.
BALTHASAR	No more words; the clerk is answered.

They move aside in the dance.

URSULA	I know you well enough: you are Signior Antonio. 95
ANTONIO	At a word, I am not.
URSULA	I know you by the waggling of your head.
ANTONIO	To tell you true, I counterfeit him.
URSULA	You could never do him so ill-well unless you were the very man. Here's his dry hand up and down. You are 100 he, you are he.
ANTONIO	At a word, I am not.
URSULA	Come, come, do you think I do not know you by your excellent wit? Can virtue hide itself? Go to, mum, you are he. Graces will appear, and there's an end. 105

They move aside in the dance.

BEATRICE	Will you not tell me who told you so?
BENEDICK	No, you shall pardon me.
BEATRICE	Nor will you not tell me who you are?
BENEDICK	Not now.
BEATRICE	That I was disdainful, and that I had my good wit out 110 of the 'Hundred Merry Tales' – well, this was Signior Benedick that said so.
BENEDICK	What's he?
BEATRICE	I am sure you know him well enough.

In their contest of wits, Beatrice gets the better of Benedick. As the dancers leave, Don John approaches Claudio and spitefully informs him that Don Pedro wants to win Hero for himself.

118–9 Only his gift: His only skill

119 libertines: scoundrels

121 villainy: rudeness

123 fleet: company
would: wish
boarded me: forced his way onto my ship

125 break a comparison: crack a joke

126 peradventure: perhaps

127–8 partridge wing: tiny bit of food

129 leaders: i.e. of the dance

132 turning: dance-step

133 amorous on: in love with

134 withdrawn: called aside

135 visor: masked person

141 birth: high rank

THINK ABOUT *for* GCSE

Performance and staging

- Do you think Beatrice knows that she is talking to Benedick (lines 106 to 132)? What are the advantages of playing the exchange as though (a) she does know, and (b) she doesn't?

Structure and form

- When addressed by Don John, Claudio pretends to be Benedick (lines 137 and 138). What then happens, which could not have happened in the same way had he revealed his true identity?

BENEDICK	Not I, believe me.	**115**
BEATRICE	Did he never make you laugh?	
BENEDICK	I pray you, what is he?	
BEATRICE	Why, he is the Prince's jester, a very dull fool. Only his gift is in devising impossible slanders. None but libertines delight in him, and the commendation is not in his wit, but in his villainy: for he both pleases men and angers them, and then they laugh at him and beat him. I am sure he is in the fleet. I would he had boarded me.	**120**
BENEDICK	When I know the gentleman, I'll tell him what you say.	
BEATRICE	Do, do. He'll but break a comparison or two on me, which, peradventure not marked or not laughed at, strikes him into melancholy. And then there's a partridge wing saved, for the fool will eat no supper that night.	**125**

Music for the dance continues.

	We must follow the leaders.	
BENEDICK	In every good thing.	**130**
BEATRICE	Nay, if they lead to any ill, I will leave them at the next turning.	

Dance continues and ends.

All exit, except DON JOHN, BORACHIO, *and* CLAUDIO.

DON JOHN	Sure my brother is amorous on Hero, and hath withdrawn her father to break with him about it. The ladies follow her and but one visor remains.	**135**
BORACHIO	And that is Claudio. I know him by his bearing.	
DON JOHN	Are not you Signior Benedick?	
CLAUDIO	You know me well: I am he.	
DON JOHN	Signior, you are very near my brother in his love. He is enamoured on Hero. I pray you dissuade him from her. She is no equal for his birth. You may do the part of an honest man in it.	**140**
CLAUDIO	How know you he loves her?	

Claudio is devastated because he thinks that Don Pedro has betrayed his trust and won Hero for himself. Benedick talks to Claudio about it.

151 **Save**: except
office: business

155 **faith**: loyalty
blood: passion
156 **accident ... proof**: common occurrence
157 **mistrusted not**: i.e. still didn't suspect

THINK ABOUT for GCSE

Themes and issues

- **Love, courtship and marriage**: What does Claudio's speech (lines 147 to 157) suggest about his attitude to love?

Characterisation

- Does Don John believe that Don Pedro is in love with Hero or is he simply trying to make trouble? Look at the conversation from line 133 to 146.

162 **willow**: symbol of unrequited love
163 **County**: Count
164 **usurer**: moneylender
chain: necklace, a symbol of wealth or status

168 **drover**: cattle-dealer

172–3 **strike ... post**: i.e. hit out at the wrong target

DON JOHN	I heard him swear his affection.
BORACHIO	So did I too, and he swore he would marry her tonight. 145
DON JOHN	Come, let us to the banquet.

Exit DON JOHN, *with* BORACHIO.

CLAUDIO	Thus answer I in name of Benedick,
	But hear these ill news with the ears of Claudio.
	'Tis certain so: the Prince woos for himself.
	Friendship is constant in all other things 150
	Save in the office and affairs of love.
	Therefore all hearts in love use their own tongues.
	Let every eye negotiate for itself,
	And trust no agent. For beauty is a witch
	Against whose charms faith melteth into blood. 155
	This is an accident of hourly proof,
	Which I mistrusted not. Farewell therefore, Hero!

Enter BENEDICK.

BENEDICK	Count Claudio?
CLAUDIO	Yea, the same.
BENEDICK	Come, will you go with me? 160
CLAUDIO	Whither?
BENEDICK	Even to the next willow, about your own business, County. What fashion will you wear the garland of? About your neck, like an usurer's chain? Or under your arm, like a lieutenant's scarf? You must wear it one way, 165 for the Prince hath got your Hero.
CLAUDIO	I wish him joy of her.
BENEDICK	Why, that's spoken like an honest drover: so they sell bullocks. But did you think the Prince would have served you thus? 170
CLAUDIO	I pray you, leave me.
BENEDICK	Ho! Now you strike like the blind man. 'Twas the boy that stole your meat, and you'll beat the post.

Benedick is angry because Beatrice has ridiculed him. Don Pedro enters and Benedick, believing that Don Pedro won Hero for himself, tells him that Claudio is heartbroken.

175 **creep into sedges**: i.e. hide

180–1 **puts … person**: assumes that everyone thinks as she does
181 **gives me out**: gives that report of me

185 **Lady Fame**: Rumour
186 **lodge … warren**: a lonely hut in a hunting park

190 **forsaken**: abandoned

THINK ABOUT *for* **GCSE**

Themes and issues

- **Noting and misunderstanding**: What has Benedick got wrong in lines 185 to 201?

Performance and staging

- If you were the director, how would you ask Benedick to act when he responds to Don Pedro (lines 185 to 201)? Should he show disapproval, for example?

---

193 **flat transgression**: simple offence

196 **a trust**: i.e. trusting another person

200 **bestowed**: used

204 **If … saying**: If they match what you say

CLAUDIO	If it will not be, I'll leave *you*.

Exit.

BENEDICK	Alas, poor hurt fowl, now will he creep into sedges! 175 But that my Lady Beatrice should know me, and not know me! The Prince's fool! Ha! It may be I go under that title because I am merry. Yea, but so I am apt to do myself wrong. I am not so reputed: it is the base, though bitter, disposition of Beatrice that puts the world into 180 her person, and so gives me out. Well, I'll be revenged as I may.

Enter DON PEDRO, *with* LEONATO *and* HERO *following.*

DON PEDRO	(*To* BENEDICK) Now signior, where's the Count? Did you see him?
BENEDICK	Troth, my lord, I have played the part of Lady Fame. 185 I found him here as melancholy as a lodge in a warren. I told him, and I think I told him true, that your Grace had got the good will of this young lady; and I offered him my company to a willow-tree, either to make him a garland, as being forsaken, or to bind him up a rod, 190 as being worthy to be whipped.
DON PEDRO	To be whipped! What's his fault?
BENEDICK	The flat transgression of a schoolboy – who being overjoyed with finding a bird's nest, shows it his companion, and he steals it. 195
DON PEDRO	Wilt thou make a trust a transgression? The transgression is in the stealer.
BENEDICK	Yet it had not been amiss the rod had been made, and the garland too: for the garland he might have worn himself, and the rod he might have bestowed on you, 200 who, as I take it, have stolen his bird's nest.
DON PEDRO	I will but teach them to sing, and restore them to the owner.
BENEDICK	If their singing answer your saying, by my faith you say honestly. 205

Benedick loudly complains about Beatrice's abuse of him. When she re-enters with Claudio, he begs Don Pedro for an excuse to leave.

206 **to**: with

209 **misused**: abused
210 **but with**: with only
211 **visor**: mask
213–4 **a great thaw**: i.e. the roads would be too muddy to allow travel
215 **conveyance**: skill
mark: target
216 **poniards**: daggers

218 **terminations**: sharp words / opinions
220 **though**: even if
220–1 **all ... transgressed**: i.e. the Garden of Eden, which Adam and Eve's sin cost them
222 **turned spit**: turned the roasting spit
cleft: split for firewood
224 **Até**: goddess of discord
good apparel: fine clothes
225 **scholar**: i.e. someone who knows Latin
conjure her: drive her away (like exorcising a ghost or evil spirit)
227 **sanctuary**: place of refuge

233 **Antipodes**: opposite side of the world

235 **Prester John**: Legendary Christian king in Africa or Asia.
236 **Cham**: emperor of China
237 **embassage**: mission / errand
238 **harpy**: A monster with a lion's body, eagle's talons and wings, and a woman's beautiful face.

THINK ABOUT for GCSE

Language

• Look at the images in lines 209 to 229. What do they reveal about the way Benedick feels about Beatrice's treatment of him?

Performance and staging

• If you were a director, what would you have Beatrice doing during lines 231 to 239?

DON PEDRO	The Lady Beatrice hath a quarrel to you: the gentleman that danced with her told her she is much wronged by you.
BENEDICK	O, she misused me past the endurance of a block! An oak but with one green leaf on it would have answered **210** her. My very visor began to assume life and scold with her. She told me, not thinking I had been myself, that I was the Prince's jester, that I was duller than a great thaw – huddling jest upon jest with such impossible conveyance upon me that I stood like a man at a mark, **215** with a whole army shooting at me. She speaks poniards, and every word stabs. If her breath were as terrible as her terminations, there were no living near her: she would infect to the north star. I would not marry her, though she were endowed with all that Adam had left **220** him before he transgressed. She would have made Hercules have turned spit, yea, and have cleft his club to make the fire too. Come, talk not of her. You shall find her the infernal Até in good apparel. I would to God some scholar would conjure her. For certainly, **225** while she is here, a man may live as quiet in hell as in a sanctuary, and people sin upon purpose because they would go thither. So indeed, all disquiet, horror, and perturbation follows her.

Enter CLAUDIO *and* BEATRICE.

DON PEDRO	Look, here she comes.	**230**
BENEDICK	Will your Grace command me any service to the world's end? I will go on the slightest errand now to the Antipodes that you can devise to send me on. I will fetch you a tooth-picker now from the furthest inch of Asia; bring you the length of Prester John's **235** foot; fetch you a hair off the great Cham's beard; do you any embassage to the Pigmies – rather than hold three words' conference with this harpy. You have no employment for me?	
DON PEDRO	None, but to desire your good company.	**240**

Beatrice hints that Benedick has broken her heart once before. She brings Claudio forward and Don Pedro explains that he has, in fact, won Hero for Claudio.

246 use: interest (monetary)

250-1 So I ... fools: i.e. I don't want Benedick to have sex with me as I would give birth to fools like him.

258 civil: polite
civil ... orange: Civil sounds like Seville.
259 complexion: Seville oranges were yellow, the colour of jealousy.
260 blazon: description
261 conceit: idea

266 all grace: the grace of God

269 were: would be

THINK ABOUT for GCSE

Relationships
• What do lines 245 to 248 suggest about Beatrice and Benedick's former relationship?

BENEDICK	O God, sir, here's a dish I love not. I cannot endure my Lady Tongue.

Exit BENEDICK.

DON PEDRO	Come, lady, come. You have lost the heart of Signior Benedick.
BEATRICE	Indeed, my lord, he lent it me awhile, and I gave him 245 use for it, a double heart for his single one. Marry, once before he won it of me with false dice: therefore your Grace may well say I have lost it.
DON PEDRO	You have put him down, lady, you have put him down.
BEATRICE	So I would not he should do me, my lord, lest I should 250 prove the mother of fools. I have brought Count Claudio, whom you sent me to seek.
DON PEDRO	Why, how now, Count! Wherefore are you sad?
CLAUDIO	Not sad, my lord.
DON PEDRO	How then? Sick? 255
CLAUDIO	Neither, my lord.
BEATRICE	The Count is neither sad, nor sick, nor merry, nor well; but civil count, civil as an orange, and something of that jealous complexion.
DON PEDRO	I' faith, lady, I think your blazon to be true; though, I'll 260 be sworn, if he be so, his conceit is false. Here, Claudio, I have wooed in thy name, and fair Hero is won. I have broke with her father, and his good will obtained. Name the day of marriage, and God give thee joy!
LEONATO	Count, take of me my daughter, and with her my 265 fortunes. His Grace hath made the match and all grace say Amen to it!
BEATRICE	Speak, Count, 'tis your cue.
CLAUDIO	Silence is the perfectest herald of joy. I were but little happy, if I could say how much. Lady, as you are mine, 270 I am yours: I give away myself for you and dote upon the exchange.

Beatrice jokingly complains that everyone in the world will get married except her. Don Pedro offers to marry her, but she politely refuses.

276 **poor fool**: a term of endearment

276–7 **windy ... care**: safe (windward) side of sorrow

277 **in his ear**: The words give a stage direction for Hero.

280 **Good ... alliance**: Thank the lord for marriage

280–1 **Thus ... world**: i.e. everyone gets married

281 **sunburnt**: unattractive

284 **getting**: offspring

291 **no matter**: nothing serious

293 **becomes**: suits

299 **cry you mercy**: beg your pardon

THINK ABOUT *for* GCSE

In the 1993 Branagh film, Don Pedro's proposal is sincere and Beatrice gently refuses.

Relationships

• How serious do you think Don Pedro's proposal is? What do you think about Beatrice's response?

Performance and staging

• In what different ways could you stage this moment?

Beatrice	Speak, cousin – or, if you cannot, stop his mouth with a kiss, and let not him speak neither.
Don Pedro	In faith, lady, you have a merry heart. 275
Beatrice	Yea, my lord; I thank it, poor fool, it keeps on the windy side of care. My cousin tells him in his ear that he is in her heart.
Claudio	And so she doth, cousin.
Beatrice	Good Lord, for alliance! Thus goes everyone to the 280 world but I, and I am sunburnt. I may sit in a corner and cry 'Heigh-ho for a husband!'
Don Pedro	Lady Beatrice, I will get you one.
Beatrice	I would rather have one of your father's getting. Hath your Grace ne'er a brother like you? Your father got 285 excellent husbands, if a maid could come by them.
Don Pedro	Will you have *me*, lady?
Beatrice	No, my lord, unless I might have another for working-days. Your Grace is too costly to wear every day. But I beseech your Grace, pardon me: I was born to speak all 290 mirth and no matter.
Don Pedro	Your silence most offends me, and to be merry best becomes you; for, out of question, you were born in a merry hour.
Beatrice	No, sure, my lord, my mother cried. But then there was 295 a star danced, and under that was I born. Cousins, God give you joy!
Leonato	Niece, will you look to those things I told you of?
Beatrice	I cry you mercy, uncle. (*To* Don Pedro) By your Grace's pardon. 300

Exit Beatrice.

Don Pedro	By my troth, a pleasant-spirited lady.

Don Pedro suggests that Beatrice would be an excellent wife for Benedick and immediately gets the support of Hero, Leonato and Claudio.

303 **sad**: 1 sad; 2 serious
     ever: always

307 **out of suit**: out of wooing her

312 **Time … crutches**: Time will drag
312–3 **till … rites**: until the marriage is consummated
314 **just**: exact

316 **answer my mind**: suit my wishes

317 **breathing**: delay

319 **interim**: meantime

322 **fain**: like to / gladly
323 **minister**: give

326 **watchings**: staying awake

329 **modest**: proper / suitable
     office: service

THINK ABOUT *for* **GCSE**

Relationships

• How well would Beatrice and Benedick be suited as husband and wife? Think about what qualities they have in common and what the differences between them are.

LEONATO	There's little of the melancholy element in her, my lord. She is never sad but when she sleeps, and not ever sad then: for I have heard my daughter say, she hath often dreamt of unhappiness and waked herself with laughing.	305
DON PEDRO	She cannot endure to hear tell of a husband.	
LEONATO	O, by no means. She mocks all her wooers out of suit.	
DON PEDRO	She were an excellent wife for Benedick.	
LEONATO	O Lord, my lord, if they were but a week married, they would talk themselves mad.	310
DON PEDRO	Count Claudio, when mean you to go to church?	
CLAUDIO	Tomorrow, my lord. Time goes on crutches till love have all his rites.	
LEONATO	Not till Monday, my dear son, which is hence a just seven-night – and a time too brief, too, to have all things answer my mind.	315
DON PEDRO	Come, you shake the head at so long a breathing – but I warrant thee, Claudio, the time shall not go dully by us. I will in the interim undertake one of Hercules' labours – which is, to bring Signior Benedick and the Lady Beatrice into a mountain of affection, the one with the other. I would fain have it a match; and I doubt not but to fashion it, if you three will but minister such assistance as I shall give you direction.	320
LEONATO	My lord, I am for you, though it cost me ten nights' watchings.	325
CLAUDIO	And I, my lord.	
DON PEDRO	And you too, gentle Hero?	
HERO	I will do any modest office, my lord, to help my cousin to a good husband.	330

Don Pedro introduces his plan to make Beatrice and Benedick fall in love.

332 strain: family

336 practise on: deceive
337 queasy stomach: distaste / squeamishness (for marriage)

THINK ABOUT for GCSE

Characterisation

- What do you know about Don Pedro so far? Think about his attitude to others and their attitudes to him.

Structure and form

- In this scene, Don John's plan to spoil the relationship between Claudio and Hero has been frustrated. Predict what Don John will do now.

Don Pedro   And Benedick is not the unhopefullest husband that I
know. Thus far can I praise him: he is of a noble strain,
of approved valour and confirmed honesty. I will teach
you how to humour your cousin, that she shall fall in
love with Benedick. And I, with your two helps, will so   335
practise on Benedick that, in despite of his quick wit and
his queasy stomach, he shall fall in love with Beatrice.
If we can do this, Cupid is no longer an archer: his glory
shall be ours, for we are the only love-gods. Go in with
me, and I will tell you my drift.   340

Exeunt.

In this scene ...

- Borachio suggests to Don John that they could convince Claudio that Hero has been unfaithful.
- Don John welcomes this plan and offers to pay Borachio for his part in it.

Don John is furious that his plan to spoil Claudio and Hero's engagement has failed. Borachio suggests another way to prevent the marriage.

3 **cross**: block / obstruct

4 **medicinable**: healing
6 **comes ... affection**: gets in the way of his desires
ranges ... mine: pleases me

THINK ABOUT for GCSE

Characterisation

- Don John does not invent the plot; Borachio does. What does that suggest about Don John?

Performance and staging

- The 1993 Branagh film has Don John creeping away from the party. Other productions have him and Borachio lurking and overhearing the wedding plans in Act 2 Scene 1. Where would you set this scene in a film version?

15 **instant**: moment

18 **temper**: mix

20 **marrying**: arranging the marriage of
21 **estimation**: worth
22 **stale**: prostitute

24 **misuse**: mislead / delude
vex: torment
25 **undo**: ruin

27 **despite**: hurt

Outside Leonato's house.

Enter DON JOHN *and* BORACHIO.

DON JOHN	It is so: the Count Claudio shall marry the daughter of Leonato.
BORACHIO	Yea, my lord, but I can cross it.
DON JOHN	Any bar, any cross, any impediment will be medicinable to me. I am sick in displeasure to him, and whatsoever comes athwart his affection ranges evenly with mine. How canst thou cross this marriage?
BORACHIO	Not honestly, my lord, but so covertly that no dishonesty shall appear in me.
DON JOHN	Show me briefly how.
BORACHIO	I think I told your lordship a year since how much I am in the favour of Margaret, the waiting-gentlewoman to Hero.
DON JOHN	I remember.
BORACHIO	I can, at any unseasonable instant of the night, appoint her to look out at her lady's chamber-window.
DON JOHN	What life is in that, to be the death of this marriage?
BORACHIO	The poison of that lies in you to temper. Go you to the Prince your brother. Spare not to tell him that he hath wronged his honour in marrying the renowned Claudio – whose estimation do you mightily hold up – to a contaminated stale, such a one as Hero.
DON JOHN	What proof shall I make of that?
BORACHIO	Proof enough to misuse the Prince, to vex Claudio, to undo Hero and kill Leonato. Look you for any other issue?
DON JOHN	Only to despite them I will endeavour anything.

5

10

15

20

25

Borachio outlines his plan to deceive Claudio and Don Pedro into believing that Hero has been unfaithful to Claudio.

28 **meet**: suitable

30 **Intend**: Pretend

33 **cozened**: tricked
33–4 **semblance ... maid**: imitation of a virgin
35 **instances**: evidence

42 **jealousy**: suspicion
43 **assurance**: certainty

46 **ducats**: Italian coins

THINK ABOUT for GCSE

Structure and form

- List the deceptions that are necessary to make Borachio's plan work. What will Don Pedro, Claudio and Leonato have to believe?
- Why is Conrade absent in this scene, do you think? Think about the differences between Don John's two henchmen.

BORACHIO Go, then: find me a meet hour to draw Don Pedro and the Count Claudio alone. Tell them that you know that Hero loves me. Intend a kind of zeal both to the Prince 30 and Claudio – as in love of your brother's honour, who hath made this match, and his friend's reputation, who is thus like to be cozened with the semblance of a maid – that you have discovered thus. They will scarcely believe this without trial. Offer them instances, 35 which shall bear no less likelihood than to see me at her chamber window, hear me call Margaret Hero, hear Margaret term me Claudio; and bring them to see this the very night before the intended wedding – for in the meantime I will so fashion the matter that Hero 40 shall be absent – and there shall appear such seeming truth of Hero's disloyalty that jealousy shall be called assurance, and all the preparation overthrown.

DON JOHN Grow this to what adverse issue it can, I will put it in practice. Be cunning in the working this, and thy fee is 45 a thousand ducats.

BORACHIO Be you constant in the accusation, and my cunning shall not shame me.

DON JOHN I will presently go learn their day of marriage.

Exeunt.

In this scene ...

- Benedick cannot understand the way a man alters when he falls in love, as Claudio has.
- Don Pedro, Leonato and Claudio enter, pretending not to see Benedick. Balthasar, one of Don Pedro's men, sings a song.
- To trick Benedick, they loudly discuss Beatrice's love for him.
- Benedick believes the whole story. When the men leave, he decides to return Beatrice's love.

Benedick is complaining about the ways in which being in love has changed Claudio.

5 **I ... already**: i.e. I'll be back instantly

11 **argument**: subject

13–14 **drum ... fife**: soldiers' musical instruments

14–15 **tabor and pipe**: small drum and flute (played in peace time)

17 **carving ... doublet**: designing the style of a new jacket

19–20 **turned orthography**: using flowery language

20 **fantastical**: bizarre

23 **oyster**: a totally silent creature, stuck in its shell

28 **grace**: good graces

THINK ABOUT for GCSE

Themes and issues

- **Men and women**: Benedick describes his ideal woman in lines 28 to 33. How far would Beatrice match his criteria?
- **Love, courtship and marriage**: What does Benedick's speech (lines 8 to 21) tell us about the typical behaviour of a lover?

Leonato's garden.

Enter BENEDICK *alone.*

BENEDICK   Boy!

Enter BOY.

BOY   Signior?

BENEDICK   In my chamber window lies a book: bring it hither to me in the orchard.

BOY   I am here already, sir.   5

BENEDICK   I know that; but I would have thee hence, and here again.

Exit BOY.

I do much wonder that one man, seeing how much another man is a fool when he dedicates his behaviours to love, will, after he hath laughed at such shallow   10
follies in others, become the argument of his own scorn by falling in love. And such a man is Claudio. I have known when there was no music with him but the drum and the fife, and now had he rather hear the tabor and the pipe. I have known when he would have walked ten   15
mile afoot to see a good armour, and now will he lie ten nights awake carving the fashion of a new doublet. He was wont to speak plain and to the purpose, like an honest man and a soldier, and now is he turned orthography: his words are a very fantastical banquet,   20
just so many strange dishes. May I be so converted and see with these eyes? I cannot tell: I think not. I will not be sworn but love may transform me to an oyster. But I'll take my oath on it, till he have made an oyster of me, he shall never make me such a fool. One woman is fair,   25
yet I am well; another is wise, yet I am well; another virtuous, yet I am well; but till all graces be in one woman, one woman shall not come in my grace. Rich she shall be, that's certain; wise, or I'll none; virtuous,

As Benedick is imagining his perfect woman, he is interrupted by the entrance of Don Pedro, Leonato and Claudio. As Benedick hides, they pretend not to have noticed him and they urge Balthasar to sing a love song.

THINK ABOUT for GCSE

Themes and issues

• **Noting and misunderstanding**: Look at lines 52 to 55. It has been said that the title of this play has several possible meanings. It can mean 'Much Ado' (a lot of fuss) over: (i) nothing, (ii) 'noting' or observing, or (iii) 'no thing' (a term for a woman's sexual organ – in other words 'a lot of fuss about women'). What instances have there been so far to support the second meaning: misunderstanding what we think we have 'noted'?

• **Men and women**: To what extent has the play so far been about attitudes to women?

30 **cheapen**: bargain for
31 **noble ... angel**: A noble was a coin worth about two-thirds as much as an angel, another coin.

40 **fit ... pennyworth**: give Benedick more than he bargained for

42 **tax**: task
43 **slander music**: give music a bad name

44 **witness still**: always a sign
45 **put ... perfection**: play down his own skill
46 **woo**: persuade

54 **crotchets**: 1 musical notes; 2 fanciful ideas

or I'll never cheapen her; fair, or I'll never look on her;   **30**
mild, or come not near me; noble, or not I for an angel;
of good discourse, an excellent musician, and her hair
shall be – of what colour it please God. Ha! The Prince
and Monsieur Love! I will hide me in the arbour.

He withdraws.

Enter Don Pedro, Leonato, *and* Claudio.

Don Pedro	Come, shall we hear this music? **35**
Claudio	Yea, my good lord. How still the evening is, As hushed on purpose to grace harmony!
Don Pedro	See you where Benedick hath hid himself?
Claudio	O very well, my lord. The music ended, We'll fit the hid fox with a pennyworth. **40**

Enter Balthasar *with musicians.*

Don Pedro	Come, Balthasar, we'll hear that song again.
Balthasar	O, good my lord, tax not so bad a voice To slander music any more than once.
Don Pedro	It is the witness still of excellency To put a strange face on his own perfection. **45** I pray thee sing, and let me woo no more.
Balthasar	Because you talk of wooing, I will sing, Since many a wooer doth commence his suit To her he thinks not worthy: yet he woos; Yet will he swear he loves.
Don Pedro	Nay, pray thee, come. **50** Or, if thou wilt hold longer argument, Do it in notes.
Balthasar	Note this before my notes: There's not a note of mine that's worth the noting.
Don Pedro	Why, these are very crotchets that he speaks; Note notes, forsooth, and nothing! **55**

Music.

Balthasar sings a song about how men can't be trusted. Benedick, in hiding, complains about the song.

57 **sheep's guts**: i.e. the strings of an instrument
hale: pull

58 **a horn ... money**: I'd rather listen to a hunting horn (another sexual joke)

66 **Hey ... nonny**: i.e. joyful sounds or songs

67 **moe**: more
68 **dumps**: sad moods
69 **fraud**: inconstancy
70 **leavy**: leafy

THINK ABOUT *for* **GCSE**

Themes and issues

- How important are the words of the song (lines 59 to 74) to the theme of **deception and disguise**?

- What do the song's lyrics tell us about romantic relationships between **men and women**?

- **Love, courtship and marriage**: The 1993 Branagh film uses the song during the opening titles. What effect does this have on the way we think about the behaviour of the lovers and the things they say about love?

77 **for a shift**: to make do

78 **An**: If
80 **bode**: foretells
had as lief: would rather
81 **night-raven**: An omen of sickness or death.

BENEDICK	(*Aside*) Now, divine air! Now is his soul ravished! Is it not strange that sheep's guts should hale souls out of men's bodies? Well, a horn for my money, when all's done.

The Song:

BALTHASAR	Sigh no more, ladies, sigh no more,	
	Men were deceivers ever,	60
	One foot in sea and one on shore,	
	To one thing constant never.	
	Then sigh not so, but let them go,	
	And be you blithe and bonny,	
	Converting all your sounds of woe	65
	Into Hey nonny, nonny.	
	Sing no more ditties, sing no moe,	
	Of dumps so dull and heavy;	
	The fraud of men was ever so,	
	Since summer first was leavy.	70
	Then sigh not so, but let them go,	
	And be you blithe and bonny,	
	Converting all your sounds of woe	
	Into Hey nonny, nonny.	
DON PEDRO	By my troth, a good song.	75
BALTHASAR	And an ill singer, my lord.	
DON PEDRO	Ha, no, no, faith: thou sing'st well enough for a shift.	
BENEDICK	(*Aside*) An he had been a dog that should have howled thus, they would have hanged him. And I pray God his bad voice bode no mischief. I had as lief have heard the night-raven, come what plague could have come after it.	80
DON PEDRO	... Yea, marry, dost thou hear, Balthasar? I pray thee, get us some excellent music; for tomorrow night we would have it at the Lady Hero's chamber window.	
BALTHASAR	The best I can, my lord.	85

To trick Benedick, Leonato,
Don Pedro and Claudio discuss
Beatrice's love for Benedick,
loudly enough for him to
overhear.

90 **stalk ... sits**: move quietly, the prey
    doesn't suspect

93 **so dote on**: be so in love with
94 **abhor**: hate

95 **Sits ... corner**: Is that how things stand

97 **enraged**: mad
98 **past ... thought**: incredible but true

99 **counterfeit**: pretend

102 **discovers**: reveals

THINK ABOUT for GCSE

Performance and staging

• Directors sometimes make a
  joke of the Boy (who
  Benedick sent on an errand
  at the beginning of this
  scene) re-entering while
  Benedick is trying to hide.
  Would you do this? If so,
  when would you have him
  come in?

Language

• Look at the imagery used in
  lines 90 and 105 to 106 to
  describe the entrapment of
  Benedick. How does it relate
  to Act 1 Scene 1, line 221?

115 **gull**: trick
116 **Knavery**: i.e. Wicked deceit

DON PEDRO	Do so; farewell.

Exit BALTHASAR.

	Come hither, Leonato. What was it you told me of today, that your niece Beatrice was in love with Signior Benedick?
CLAUDIO	(*Aside*) O, ay; stalk on, stalk on, the fowl sits. (*Aloud*) I 90 did never think that lady would have loved any man.
LEONATO	No, nor I neither; but most wonderful that she should so dote on Signior Benedick, whom she hath in all outward behaviours seemed ever to abhor.
BENEDICK	(*Aside*) Is't possible? Sits the wind in *that* corner? 95
LEONATO	By my troth, my lord, I cannot tell what to think of it: but that she loves him with an enraged affection – it is past the infinite of thought.
DON PEDRO	Maybe she doth but counterfeit.
CLAUDIO	Faith, like enough. 100
LEONATO	O God! Counterfeit? There was never counterfeit of passion came so near the life of passion as she discovers it.
DON PEDRO	Why, what effects of passion shows she?
CLAUDIO	(*To* DON PEDRO *and* LEONATO) Bait the hook well: this fish 105 will bite.
LEONATO	What effects, my lord? She will sit you – you heard my daughter tell you how.
CLAUDIO	She did, indeed.
DON PEDRO	How, how, I pray you? You amaze me. I would have 110 thought her spirit had been invincible against all assaults of affection.
LEONATO	I would have sworn it had, my lord, especially against Benedick.
BENEDICK	(*Aside*) I should think this a gull, but that the white- 115 bearded fellow speaks it. Knavery cannot, sure, hide himself in such reverence.

Don Pedro, Claudio and Leonato describe how desperate Beatrice is because Benedick does not love her back.

119 **Hold**: Keep

127 **smock**: undergarment

132 **sheet**: Here, also a bed sheet.

134 **halfpence**: tiny bits

136 **flout**: ridicule

THINK ABOUT for GCSE

Characterisation

• Why doesn't Benedick realise that the men aren't telling the truth about Beatrice? What does that suggest about his feelings for her?

142 **ecstasy**: madness

144 **outrage**: violence

Performance and staging

• If you were the director, how would you stage this scene? Think about what sort of set would be needed.

150 **alms**: good deed

CLAUDIO	(*To* DON PEDRO *and* LEONATO) He hath ta'en the infection. Hold it up.
DON PEDRO	Hath she made her affection known to Benedick? 120
LEONATO	No, and swears she never will: that's her torment.
CLAUDIO	'Tis true, indeed, so your daughter says. 'Shall I,' says she, 'that have so oft encountered him with scorn, write to him that I love him?'
LEONATO	This says she now when she is beginning to write to 125 him; for she'll be up twenty times a night, and there will she sit in her smock till she have writ a sheet of paper. My daughter tells us all.
CLAUDIO	Now you talk of a sheet of paper, I remember a pretty jest your daughter told us of. 130
LEONATO	O, when she had writ it and was reading it over, she found 'Benedick' and 'Beatrice' between the sheet?
CLAUDIO	That.
LEONATO	O, she tore the letter into a thousand halfpence – railed at herself that she should be so immodest to write to one 135 that she knew would flout her. 'I measure him,' says she, 'by my own spirit; for I should flout him if he writ to me: yea, though I love him, I should.'
CLAUDIO	Then down upon her knees she falls – weeps, sobs, beats her heart, tears her hair, prays, curses – 'O sweet 140 Benedick! God give me patience!'
LEONATO	She doth indeed; my daughter says so. And the ecstasy hath so much overborne her that my daughter is sometime afeard she will do a desperate outrage to herself. It is very true. 145
DON PEDRO	It were good that Benedick knew of it by some other, if she will not discover it.
CLAUDIO	To what end? He would make but a sport of it, and torment the poor lady worse.
DON PEDRO	An he should, it were an alms to hang him. She's an 150 excellent sweet lady, and, out of all suspicion, she is virtuous.

The men express their sympathy for Beatrice and criticism of Benedick if he does not return her love.

155 **blood**: passion
156 **ten ... one**: i.e. the odds are very good

159 **dotage**: adoration
160 **daffed**: put aside
made ... myself: married her

166 **bate**: lessen
accustomed: customary
167 **tender**: offer

169 **contemptible**: scoffing

170 **proper**: handsome

171 **hath ... happiness**: i.e. is good-looking enough

175 **Hector**: the most valiant of the Trojan warriors
176 **quarrels**: duels

THINK ABOUT for GCSE

Characterisation

• Which of the men's statements about Benedick are true and which are intended to wind him up?

---

183 **howsoever**: even though
183–4 **some ... make**: the rude jokes he tells

CLAUDIO	And she is exceeding wise.
DON PEDRO	In everything but in loving Benedick.
LEONATO	O, my lord, wisdom and blood combating in so tender 155 a body, we have ten proofs to one that blood hath the victory. I am sorry for her, as I have just cause, being her uncle and her guardian.
DON PEDRO	I would she had bestowed this dotage on me. I would have daffed all other respects and made her half myself. 160 I pray you, tell Benedick of it, and hear what he will say.
LEONATO	Were it good, think you?
CLAUDIO	Hero thinks surely she will die: for she says she will die if he love her not. And she will die ere she make her love known. And she will die, if he woo her, rather than 165 she will bate one breath of her accustomed crossness.
DON PEDRO	She doth well. If she should make tender of her love, 'tis very possible he'll scorn it: for the man, as you know all, hath a contemptible spirit.
CLAUDIO	He is a very proper man. 170
DON PEDRO	He hath, indeed, a good outward happiness.
CLAUDIO	Before God, and in my mind, very wise.
DON PEDRO	He doth, indeed, show some sparks that are like wit.
CLAUDIO	And I take him to be valiant.
DON PEDRO	As Hector, I assure you. And in the managing of 175 quarrels you may say he is wise: for either he avoids them with great discretion, or undertakes them with a most Christian-like fear.
LEONATO	If he do fear God, 'a must necessarily keep peace. If he break the peace, he *ought* to enter into a quarrel with 180 fear and trembling.
DON PEDRO	And so will he do, for the man doth fear God – howsoever it seems not in him by some large jests he will make. Well, I am sorry for your niece. Shall we go seek Benedick, and tell him of her love? 185

The men discuss whether their scheme will be successful. Benedick begins to consider his feelings for Beatrice.

186 wear it out: get over it in time

198–9 they ... dotage: each one believes that the other is in love with them
199 no such matter: that isn't the case
200–1 dumb-show: mime

THINK ABOUT for GCSE

Structure and form

• Don Pedro imagines that when Beatrice and Benedick meet, these two witty people will not be able to think of a word to say (lines 198 to 201). What do you think will happen when Benedick next meets Beatrice?

Characterisation

• Benedick has an instant change of heart. What does this suggest about his earlier statements about marriage and his earlier criticisms of Beatrice?

203 sadly: seriously
204–5 have ... bent: are stretched to the limit
205 requited: returned
206 censured: criticised

210 detractions: bad points

213 reprove: disprove
214 argument: proof

216 quirks: jokes

220–1 Shall ... humour?: i.e. Should a man be put off what he wants to do by a few cheap jokes and wise sayings?

CLAUDIO	Never tell him, my lord. Let her wear it out with good counsel.
LEONATO	Nay, that's impossible. She may wear her heart out first.
DON PEDRO	Well, we will hear further of it by your daughter: let it cool the while. I love Benedick well. And I could wish **190** he would modestly examine himself, to see how much he is unworthy so good a lady.
LEONATO	My lord, will you walk? Dinner is ready.
CLAUDIO	(*Aside*) If he do not dote on her upon this, I will never trust my expectation. **195**
DON PEDRO	(*Aside to* LEONATO) Let there be the same net spread for her; and that must your daughter and her gentlewomen carry. The sport will be, when they hold one an opinion of another's dotage – and no such matter. That's the scene that I would see, which will be merely a dumb- **200** show. Let us send her to call him in to dinner.

Exit DON PEDRO, *with* CLAUDIO *and* LEONATO.

| BENEDICK | (***Coming forward***) This can be no trick. The conference was sadly borne. They have the truth of this from Hero. They seem to pity the lady: it seems her affections have their full bent. Love me? Why, it must be requited. I **205** hear how I am censured: they say I will bear myself proudly, if I perceive the love come from her. They say, too, that she will rather die than give any sign of affection. I did never think to marry. I must not seem proud: happy are they that hear their detractions and **210** can put them to mending. They say the lady is fair – 'tis a truth, I can bear them witness; and virtuous – 'tis so, I cannot reprove it; and wise – but for loving me. By my troth, it is no addition to her wit, nor no great argument of her folly – for I will be horribly in love with her. I **215** may chance have some odd quirks and remnants of wit broken on me, because I have railed so long against marriage. But doth not the appetite alter? A man loves the meat in his youth that he cannot endure in his age. Shall quips and sentences and these paper bullets of the **220** brain awe a man from the career of his humour? No: the |

Benedick is amazed to discover that he loves Beatrice. She arrives to ask Benedick to come in to dinner and is puzzled by his strange behaviour.

THINK ABOUT for GCSE

Context

- Benedick's statement 'If I do not love her, I am a Jew' (line 240) strikes modern audiences as anti-Semitic. In Shakespeare's time people were routinely anti-Jewish. What should a modern production do with this line? What are the arguments for and against cutting it, changing it, or leaving it as it is?

Performance and staging

- If you were a director, how would you deal with this in a production? Would you cut the line, change it or leave it as it is? Why?

233 **daw**: jackdaw (thought to be a foolish bird)
withal: with
have no stomach: are obviously not hungry

240 **Jew**: Often a term of abuse in Shakespeare's time.

world must be peopled. When I said I would die a
bachelor, I did not think I should live till I were married.
Here comes Beatrice. By this day, she's a fair lady! I do
spy some marks of love in her.   **225**

Enter BEATRICE.

BEATRICE   Against my will I am sent to bid you come in to
                 dinner.

BENEDICK   Fair Beatrice, I thank you for your pains.

BEATRICE   I took no more pains for those thanks than you take
                 pains to thank me. If it had been painful I would not
                 have come.   **230**

BENEDICK   You take pleasure then in the message?

BEATRICE   Yea, just so much as you may take upon a knife's point,
                 and choke a daw withal. You have no stomach, signior.
                 Fare you well.

                                                          Exit.

BENEDICK   Ha! 'Against my will I am sent to bid you come in to **235**
                 dinner'– there's a double meaning in that. 'I took no
                 more pains for those thanks than you took pains to
                 thank me'– that's as much as to say, 'Any pains that I
                 take for you is as easy as thanks.' If I do not take pity of
                 her, I am a villain! If I do not love her, I am a Jew. I will **240**
                 go get her picture.

                                                          Exit.

In this scene ...

- Hero asks Margaret to tell Beatrice that she and Ursula are talking about Beatrice in the garden.
- Ursula and Hero stand near to where Beatrice is hiding and discuss Benedick's love for Beatrice and the fact that she does not return it.
- Beatrice is dismayed to realise how proud and scornful she seems to others.
- Beatrice resolves to return Benedick's love.

Margaret goes to find Beatrice to tell her that Hero and Ursula are in the garden, talking about her. Believing her, Beatrice hides where she can hear their conversation.

3   **Proposing**: talking

7   **pleachèd**: with branches twisted around each other
9   **favourites**: favoured courtiers

11   **power**: i.e. of the princes
12   **propose**: conversation
     office: responsibility

14   **presently**: immediately

16   **trace**: tread

23   **hearsay**: rumour

24   **lapwing**: A bird which stays low to the ground to escape notice.

THINK ABOUT for GCSE

Performance and staging

- Hero's speeches offer some details to the set designer. What sort of scenery does this scene require on a modern stage? Where is Beatrice expected to hide?

Leonato's garden.

Enter HERO *and her two gentlewomen,* MARGARET *and* URSULA.

HERO	Good Margaret, run thee to the parlour.
	There shalt thou find my cousin Beatrice
	Proposing with the Prince and Claudio.
	Whisper her ear, and tell her I and Ursula
	Walk in the orchard, and our whole discourse 5
	Is all of her. Say that thou overheard'st us,
	And bid her steal into the pleachèd bower,
	Where honeysuckles, ripened by the sun,
	Forbid the sun to enter – like favourites,
	Made proud by princes, that advance their pride 10
	Against that power that bred it. There will she hide her,
	To listen our propose. This is thy office:
	Bear thee well in it, and leave us alone.
MARGARET	I'll make her come, I warrant you, presently.

Exit.

HERO	Now Ursula, when Beatrice doth come, 15
	As we do trace this alley up and down,
	Our talk must only be of Benedick.
	When I do name him, let it be thy part
	To praise him more than ever man did merit.
	My talk to thee must be how Benedick 20
	Is sick in love with Beatrice. Of this matter
	Is little Cupid's crafty arrow made,
	That only wounds by hearsay. Now begin –

Enter BEATRICE, *trying not to be seen: she slips into hiding.*

	– For look where Beatrice like a lapwing runs
	Close by the ground, to hear our conference. 25

Ursula and Hero loudly discuss Benedick's love for Beatrice and Beatrice's scorn for men in general.

27 oars: fins

30 couchèd: hidden
woodbine coverture: cover of honeysuckle

35 coy: stand-offish / distant
36 haggards: wild hawks

38 my ... lord: my fiancé

42 wish him: advise him to

45 as full ... bed: i.e. as happy a marriage
46 couch: lie

52 Misprizing: undervaluing

54 All matter else: i.e. everyone else's wit
55 take ... affection: understand the idea of being in love
56 self-endeared: in love with herself

THINK ABOUT for GCSE

Language

- Find the animal imagery in lines 24 to 36. How does this compare with the language used about the trapping of Benedick in Act 2 Scene 3?

Themes and issues

- **Men and women**: In what ways is Hero's condemnation of Beatrice similar to the men's condemnation of Benedick in Act 2 Scene 3?

URSULA	(*To* HERO) The pleasant'st angling is to see the fish
	Cut with her golden oars the silver stream,
	And greedily devour the treacherous bait.
	So angle we for Beatrice, who even now
	Is couchèd in the woodbine coverture. 30
	Fear you not my part of the dialogue.
HERO	(*To* URSULA) Then go we near her, that her ear lose
	nothing
	Of the false sweet bait that we lay for it.

They approach BEATRICE*'s hiding-place.*

	(*Aloud*) No, truly, Ursula, she is too disdainful.
	I know her spirits are as coy and wild 35
	As haggards of the rock.
URSULA	But are you sure
	That Benedick loves Beatrice so entirely?
HERO	So says the Prince and my new-trothèd lord.
URSULA	And did they bid you tell her of it, madam?
HERO	They did entreat me to acquaint her of it. 40
	But I persuaded them, if they loved Benedick,
	To wish him wrestle with affection,
	And never to let Beatrice know of it.
URSULA	Why did you so? Doth not the gentleman
	Deserve as full as fortunate a bed 45
	As ever Beatrice shall couch upon?
HERO	O god of love! I know he doth deserve
	As much as may be yielded to a man.
	But Nature never framed a woman's heart
	Of prouder stuff than that of Beatrice. 50
	Disdain and scorn ride sparkling in her eyes,
	Misprizing what they look on, and her wit
	Values itself so highly that to her
	All matter else seems weak. She cannot love,
	Nor take no shape nor project of affection, 55
	She is so self-endeared.

Hero says that she will advise Benedick to get over his love for Beatrice. Playing along, Ursula suggests that Hero is being too hard on Beatrice.

57   **were not**: would not be

60   **How**: no matter how
rarely featured: handsome

61   **spell him backward**: turn his virtues into faults

63   **black**: of a dark complexion
antic: grotesque clown

64   **lance ill-headed**: badly-tipped spear

65   **low**: short
agate: Small ornamental stone, often carved with images of people.

70   **simpleness**: sincerity
purchaseth: deserve

71   **carping**: criticising

72   **odd … fashions**: over-particular

76   **press … death**: torture

78   **Consume … sighs**: Referring to the belief that each sigh costs the heart one drop of blood.

79   **were**: would be

84   **honest**: harmless

THINK ABOUT *for* GCSE

Characterisation

• What qualities of Beatrice do the women criticise (lines 49 to 80)? How fair are their criticisms, from what you have seen of Beatrice so far?

Performance and staging

• Directors usually try to make this scene different from Act 2 Scene 3. How would you stage it?

URSULA	Sure, I think so;
	And therefore, certainly, it were not good
	She knew his love, lest she'll make sport at it.
HERO	Why, you speak truth. I never yet saw man,
	How wise, how noble, young, how rarely featured, **60**
	But she would spell him backward. If fair-faced,
	She would swear the gentleman should be her sister;
	If black, why, Nature, drawing of an antic,
	Made a foul blot; if tall, a lance ill-headed;
	If low, an agate very vilely cut; **65**
	If speaking, why, a vane blown with all winds;
	If silent, why, a block movèd with none.
	So turns she every man the wrong side out,
	And never gives to truth and virtue that
	Which simpleness and merit purchaseth. **70**
URSULA	Sure, sure, such carping is not commendable.
HERO	No; not to be so odd and from all fashions,
	As Beatrice is, cannot be commendable.
	But who dare tell her so? If I should speak,
	She would mock me into air. O, she would laugh me **75**
	Out of myself, press me to death with wit!
	Therefore let Benedick, like covered fire,
	Consume away in sighs, waste inwardly.
	It were a better death than die with mocks,
	Which is as bad as die with tickling. **80**
URSULA	Yet tell her of it: hear what she will say.
HERO	No: rather I will go to Benedick
	And counsel him to fight against his passion.
	And, truly, I'll devise some honest slanders
	To stain my cousin with. One doth not know **85**
	How much an ill word may empoison liking.
URSULA	O, do not do your cousin such a wrong!
	She cannot be so much without true judgement –
	Having so swift and excellent a wit
	As she is prized to have – as to refuse **90**
	So rare a gentleman as Signior Benedick.

When Beatrice is left alone, she declares that she will change her proud ways and return Benedick's love.

THINK ABOUT for GCSE

Language

• Lines 35 to 36 and line 112 both say that Beatrice is like a wild bird who will be tamed by Benedick. What is the effect in this scene of the hawk-taming imagery? What is the effect if we recall Don Pedro's observation from Act 1 Scene 1, lines 221 to 222?)

Themes and issues

• **Love, courtship and marriage**: There are several references to Cupid in this scene (look at lines 21 to 23 and 106). How do the characters describe Cupid throughout the play? Is love a matter of chance, or is it arranged by others?

• In what ways has this scene contributed to the theme of **noting and misunderstanding**?

92 **only**: the best

96 **argument**: conversational skill

98 **name**: reputation

101 **every day tomorrow**: i.e. every day of my life, starting tomorrow

102 **attires**: head-dresses

104 **limed**: trapped

105 **haps**: chance

107 **fire … ears**: Referring to the idea that your ears burn when someone talks about you.

110 **No … such**: No-one speaks well of proud people behind their backs

116 **better … reportingly**: more than by hearsay

HERO	He is the only man of Italy –
	Always excepted my dear Claudio.

URSULA   I pray you be not angry with me, madam,
Speaking my fancy: Signior Benedick,   95
For shape, for bearing, argument and valour,
Goes foremost in report through Italy.

HERO   Indeed, he hath an excellent good name.

URSULA   His excellence did earn it ere he had it.
When are you married, madam?   100

HERO   Why, every day tomorrow! Come, go in.
I'll show thee some attires, and have thy counsel
Which is the best to furnish me tomorrow.

URSULA   (*To* HERO) She's limed, I warrant you: we have caught
her, madam.

HERO   (*To* URSULA) If it prove so, then loving goes by haps: 105
Some Cupid kills with arrows, some with traps.

Exit HERO, *with* URSULA.

BEATRICE   (*Coming forward*) What fire is in mine ears? Can this
be true?
Stand I condemned for pride and scorn so much?
Contempt, farewell! and maiden pride, adieu!
No glory lives behind the back of such.   110
And Benedick, love on. I will requite thee,
Taming my wild heart to thy loving hand.
If thou dost love, my kindness shall incite thee
To bind our loves up in a holy band.
For others say thou dost deserve, and I   115
Believe it better than reportingly.

Exit.

In this scene ...

- Don Pedro, Claudio and Leonato tease Benedick about how his behaviour and appearance have altered.
- They congratulate one another on the success of their plan to make Benedick fall in love with Beatrice.
- Don John tells Don Pedro and Claudio that he has proof that Hero has been unfaithful to Claudio.

Don Pedro, Claudio and Leonato tease Benedick about his changed behaviour and appearance.

THINK ABOUT for GCSE

Performance and staging

- In the 1993 Branagh film, Benedick is shown preening himself in front of a mirror. In what other ways could an actor show the change in his behaviour?

Characterisation

- Which qualities of Benedick's is Don Pedro making fun of?

3 **vouchsafe**: allow

6 **only be bold with**: i.e. take only

9 **hangman**: i.e. rascal

14 **sadder**: more serious

17 **wants**: lacks

19 **toothache**: frequently associated with love-sickness
20 **Draw it**: Pull it out
21 **Hang it**: Curse it
22 **hang ... afterwards**: A reference to executions in which the victim was hung, drawn and quartered.
24 **Where ... worm**: Toothaches were supposedly caused by imbalances of bodily fluids or by worms.

ACT 3   SCENE 2

At Leonato's house.

Enter DON PEDRO, CLAUDIO, BENEDICK *and* LEONATO.

DON PEDRO	I do but stay till your marriage be consummate, and then go I toward Aragon.
CLAUDIO	I'll bring you thither, my lord, if you'll vouchsafe me.
DON PEDRO	Nay, that would be as great a soil in the new gloss of your marriage as to show a child his new coat and 5 forbid him to wear it. I will only be bold with Benedick for his company; for, from the crown of his head to the sole of his foot, he is all mirth. He hath twice or thrice cut Cupid's bow-string and the little hangman dare not shoot at him. He hath a heart as sound as a bell and 10 his tongue is the clapper – for what his heart thinks, his tongue speaks.
BENEDICK	Gallants, I am not as I have been.
LEONATO	So say I: methinks you are sadder.
CLAUDIO	I hope he be in love. 15
DON PEDRO	Hang him, truant! There's no true drop of blood in him to be truly touched with love. If he be sad, he wants money.
BENEDICK	I have the toothache.
DON PEDRO	Draw it. 20
BENEDICK	Hang it!
CLAUDIO	You must hang it first, and draw it afterwards.
DON PEDRO	What! Sigh for the toothache?
LEONATO	Where is but a humour or a worm.
BENEDICK	Well, everyone can master a grief but he that has it. 25
CLAUDIO	Yet say I, he is in love.

The men try to get Benedick to admit that he is in love.

27–8 fancy … fancy: infatuation … fad

28 disguises: outfits / costumes

31 slops: loose breeches

36 old: customary
'A: He
o' mornings: every morning

40–1 old … tennis-balls: Tennis balls were stuffed with hair in Elizabethan times.

44 civet: perfume

47 note: sign

48 wont: accustomed

49 paint himself: wear cosmetics

52 lute-string: Lutes were used to play love songs.
governed by stops: regulated by frets (on a lute)

THINK ABOUT for GCSE

Characterisation

• How did Benedick look before and how does he look now? Looking at lines 27 to 37 in particular, think about how his clothes and facial appearance might have changed now that he is in love.

58 ill conditions: bad qualities

DON PEDRO	There is no appearance of fancy in him, unless it be a fancy that he hath to strange disguises – as to be a Dutchman today, a Frenchman tomorrow, or in the shape of two countries at once, as a German from the 30 waist downward, all slops, and a Spaniard from the hip upward, no doublet. Unless he have a fancy to this foolery, as it appears he hath, he is no fool for fancy, as you would have it appear he is.
CLAUDIO	If he be not in love with some woman, there is no 35 believing old signs. 'A brushes his hat o' mornings: what should that bode?
DON PEDRO	Hath any man seen him at the barber's?
CLAUDIO	No – but the barber's man hath been seen with him, and the old ornament of his cheek hath already stuffed 40 tennis-balls.
LEONATO	Indeed, he looks younger than he did, by the loss of a beard.
DON PEDRO	Nay, 'a rubs himself with civet: can you smell him out by that? 45
CLAUDIO	That's as much as to say, the sweet youth's in love.
DON PEDRO	The greatest note of it is his melancholy.
CLAUDIO	And when was he wont to wash his face?
DON PEDRO	Yea, or to paint himself? For the which, I hear what they say of him. 50
CLAUDIO	Nay, but his jesting spirit, which is now crept into a lute-string, and now governed by stops.
DON PEDRO	Indeed, that tells a heavy tale for him. Conclude, conclude: he is in love.
CLAUDIO	Nay, but I know who loves him. 55
DON PEDRO	That would I know too. I warrant, one that knows him not.
CLAUDIO	Yes, and his ill conditions; and, in despite of all, dies for him.

Benedick takes Leonato aside to speak to him. Don John arrives to see Don Pedro and Claudio. He seems concerned about the marriage between Claudio and Hero.

THINK ABOUT for GCSE

Language

- 'Dies' (in line 58) also meant 'has an orgasm'. How does Don Pedro's reply (line 60) show that he has picked up the *double-entendre* (double meaning)?

- How do you feel about this exchange? Think about whether you find it funny or crude, for example.

Characterisation

- How does it affect your impressions of Don Pedro and Claudio?

Themes and issues

- **Men and women:** What does their exchange reveal about male attitudes to women?

61   **charm**: cure

63   **hobby-horses**: buffoons

65   **break**: talk

70   **e'en**: evening
71   **If ... served**: If you are free

80   **discover**: reveal

82   **aim better at**: think better of
83   **manifest**: make plain
84   **holp**: helped

87–8   **circumstances shortened**: to cut a long story short

90

DON PEDRO   She shall be buried with her face upwards.   **60**

BENEDICK   Yet is this no charm for the toothache. (*To* LEONATO) Old signior, walk aside with me. I have studied eight or nine wise words to speak to you, which these hobby-horses must not hear.

Exit BENEDICK, *with* LEONATO.

DON PEDRO   For my life, to break with him about Beatrice.   **65**

CLAUDIO   'Tis even so. Hero and Margaret have by this played their parts with Beatrice; and then the two bears will not bite one another when they meet.

Enter DON JOHN.

DON JOHN   My lord and brother, God save you!

DON PEDRO   Good-e'en, brother.   **70**

DON JOHN   If your leisure served, I would speak with you.

DON PEDRO   In private?

DON JOHN   If it please you. Yet Count Claudio may hear, for what I would speak of concerns him.

DON PEDRO   What's the matter?   **75**

DON JOHN   (*To* CLAUDIO) Means your lordship to be married tomorrow?

DON PEDRO   You know he does.

DON JOHN   I know not that, when he knows what I know.

CLAUDIO   If there be any impediment, I pray you discover it.   **80**

DON JOHN   (*To* CLAUDIO) You may think I love you not. Let that appear hereafter, and aim better at me by that I now will manifest. For my brother, I think he holds you well, and in dearness of heart hath holp to effect your ensuing marriage – surely suit ill spent, and labour ill bestowed!   **85**

DON PEDRO   Why, what's the matter?

DON JOHN   I came hither to tell you – and, circumstances shortened, for she has been too long a talking of, the lady is disloyal.

Don John says that he has proof that Hero has been unfaithful to Claudio. He invites Don Pedro and Claudio to see the evidence that night.

94 **paint out**: describe

96 **Wonder ... warrant**: Don't try to puzzle it out until you have seen more proof.

THINK ABOUT
for GCSE

Characterisation

- Claudio is young and sometimes seems to rely on Don Pedro's judgement rather than on his own (look at Act 1 Scene 1, lines 244 to 282). How does Don John exploit that in this scene?

Themes and issues

- **Men and women**: Which parts of this scene reinforce the idea that this play is 'Much Ado About' attitudes to women? (See also 'Themes and issues' questions on page 64.)

- **Noting and misunderstanding**: Which parts of this scene suggest that it is more 'Much Ado About' noting? (Look especially at lines 103 to 104.)

103 **confess not**: don't admit

108 **in the congregation**: among the people gathered for the wedding

112 **disparage**: insult
113 **Bear it coldly**: Keep calm

115 **untowardly turned**: turned out for the worst
116 **mischief ... thwarting**: evil striking unexpectedly

Claudio	Who? Hero?	**90**
Don John	Even she – Leonato's Hero, your Hero: every man's Hero.	
Claudio	Disloyal?	
Don John	The word is too good to paint out her wickedness. I could say she were worse: think you of a worse title, and I will fit her to it. Wonder not till further warrant. Go but with me tonight, you shall see her chamber-window entered, even the night before her wedding-day. If you love her then, tomorrow wed her. But it would better fit your honour to change your mind.	**95** **100**
Claudio	May this be so?	
Don Pedro	I will not think it.	
Don John	If you dare not trust that you see, confess not that you know. If you will follow me, I will show you enough. And when you have seen more and heard more, proceed accordingly.	**105**
Claudio	If I see anything tonight why I should not marry her, tomorrow in the congregation, where I should wed, there will I shame her.	
Don Pedro	And, as I wooed for thee to obtain her, I will join with thee to disgrace her.	**110**
Don John	I will disparage her no farther till you are my witnesses. Bear it coldly but till midnight, and let the issue show itself.	
Don Pedro	O day untowardly turned!	**115**
Claudio	O mischief strangely thwarting!	
Don John	O plague right well prevented! So will you say when you have seen the sequel.	

Exeunt.

In this scene ...

- The bumbling Dogberry and Verges inform the Watch of their duties.
- Borachio brags to Conrade that he has earned money from Don John for dishonouring Hero.
- Despite not being very good at their job, the Watch manage to arrest Borachio and Conrade.

s.d.   **Watch**: part-time police
1   **true**: honest
2   **salvation**: He means 'damnation'.

7   **give ... charge**: describe their duties
8   **desertless**: He means 'deserving'.
9   **constable**: head of the watch patrol (Dogberry is Master Constable)

13   **well-favoured**: handsome

THINK ABOUT *for* **GCSE**

Language

- Dogberry is a master of malapropisms (using the wrong word). What examples are there in this scene (lines 1 to 84) of words which mean the opposite of what he intends?

Performance and staging

- What opportunities for visual or physical comedy are there at the opening of this scene? For example, what do these characters look like? How do they behave?

20   **senseless**: He means 'sensible'.
22   **comprehend ... vagrom ...**: He means 'apprehend' ... 'vagrant' ...
23   **stand**: stop
24   **'a**: he

Near Leonato's house.

Enter Dogberry *and his partner* Verges, *with men of the Watch.*

Dogberry	Are you good men and true?
Verges	Yea, or else it were pity but they should suffer salvation, body and soul.
Dogberry	Nay, that were a punishment too good for them, if they should have any allegiance in them, being chosen for 5 the Prince's watch.
Verges	Well, give them their charge, neighbour Dogberry.
Dogberry	First, who think you the most desertless man to be constable?
Watchman 1	Hugh Oatcake, sir, or George Seacoal, for they can 10 write and read.
Dogberry	Come hither, neighbour Seacoal. God hath blessed you with a good name. To be a well-favoured man is the gift of fortune; but to write and read comes by nature.
Watchman 2	Both which, Master Constable – 15
Dogberry	You have. I knew it would be your answer. Well, for your favour, sir, why, give God thanks, and make no boast of it; and for your writing and reading, let that appear when there is no need of such vanity. You are thought here to be the most senseless and fit man for the 20 constable of the watch: therefore bear you the lantern. This is your charge: you shall comprehend all vagrom men – you are to bid any man stand, in the Prince's name.
Watchman 2	How if 'a will not stand?
Dogberry	Why, then, take no note of him, but let him go – and 25 presently call the rest of the watch together and thank God you are rid of a knave.

Dogberry gives the Watch their instructions.

30   **meddle**: deal

32   **tolerable**: He means 'intolerable' (cannot be suffered).

34–5   **belongs to**: is appropriate for

36   **ancient**: experienced

38   **bills**: weapons

THINK ABOUT for GCSE

Language

- Find the word-play in Dogberry's speech (lines 52 to 55). Do you think he intends the pun?

Performance and staging

- From what you have seen of Dogberry so far, what sort of actor would you cast in the role if you were the director?

52–3   **they … defiled**: i.e. if you associate with bad people you pick up their bad ways

53   **pitch**: tar

60   **still**: quieten

VERGES	If he will not stand when he is bidden, he is none of the Prince's subjects.
DOGBERRY	True, and they are to meddle with none but the Prince's subjects. You shall also make no noise in the streets: for, for the watch to babble and to talk is most tolerable and not to be endured.
WATCHMAN 1	We will rather sleep than talk. We know what belongs to a watch.
DOGBERRY	Why, you speak like an ancient and most quiet watchman, for I cannot see how sleeping should offend – only have a care that your bills be not stolen. Well, you are to call at all the ale-houses, and bid those that are drunk get them to bed.
WATCHMAN 2	How if they will not?
DOGBERRY	Why, then, let them alone till they are sober. If they make you not then the better answer, you may say they are not the men you took them for.
WATCHMAN 2	Well, sir.
DOGBERRY	If you meet a thief, you may suspect him, by virtue of your office, to be no true man. And, for such kind of men, the less you meddle or make with them, why, the more is for your honesty.
WATCHMAN 2	If we know him to be a thief, shall we not lay hands on him?
DOGBERRY	Truly, by your office you may, but I think they that touch pitch will be defiled. The most peaceable way for you, if you *do* take a thief, is to let him show himself what he is and steal out of your company.
VERGES	You have been always called a merciful man, partner.
DOGBERRY	Truly, I would not hang a dog by my will, much more a man who hath any honesty in him.
VERGES	If you hear a child cry in the night, you must call to the nurse and bid her still it.

Line numbers: 30, 35, 40, 45, 50, 55, 60

Dogberry and Verges leave
the watchmen to their duties,
having asked them to keep
an eye on Leonato's house.
Conrade and Borachio enter
and the watchmen overhear
their conversation.

67   **present**: represent
68   **stay**: detain

70   **Five ... on't**: I'll bet five to one

75–6   **An ... chances**: If anything serious
       happens
76–7   **Keep ... own**: i.e. Be discreet

83   **coil**: fuss
84   **vigitant**: He means 'vigilant'.

THINK ABOUT for GCSE

Context

• In Shakespeare's time town
  constables and watchmen
  were often considered
  a joke because of their
  incompetence. What is your
  impression of the Watch so
  far?

89   **Mass**: By the Mass (an oath)
90   **scab**: Also means 'villain'.

Watchman 2	How if the nurse be asleep and will not hear us?
Dogberry	Why, then, depart in peace, and let the child wake her with crying: for the ewe that will not hear her lamb when it baas will never answer a calf when he bleats.
Verges	'Tis very true.
Dogberry	This is the end of the charge. You, constable, are to present the Prince's own person. If you meet the Prince in the night, you may stay him.
Verges	Nay, by'r Lady, that I think 'a cannot.
Dogberry	Five shillings to one on't, with any man that knows the statutes: he may stay him. Marry, not without the Prince be willing – for, indeed, the watch ought to offend no man, and it is an offence to stay a man against his will.
Verges	By'r Lady, I think it be so.
Dogberry	Ha, ah ha! Well, masters, good night. An there be any matter of weight chances, call up me. Keep your fellows' counsels and your own, and good night. Come, neighbour.
Watchman 1	Well, masters, we hear our charge. Let us go sit here upon the church-bench till two, and then all to bed.
Dogberry	One word more, honest neighbours. I pray you, watch about Signior Leonato's door – for the wedding being there tomorrow, there is a great coil tonight. Adieu: be vigitant, I beseech you.

Exit Dogberry, *with* Verges.

Enter Borachio *and* Conrade.

Borachio	What, Conrade!
Watchman 2	(*Aside*) Peace! Stir not.
Borachio	Conrade, I say!
Conrade	Here, man; I am at thy elbow.
Borachio	Mass, and my elbow itched: I thought there would a scab follow.

Line numbers: 65, 70, 75, 80, 85, 90

Borachio promises to share some secret information with Conrade.

93 **Stand thee close**: Stay hidden
pent-house: roof overhang
94 **true drunkard**: The name 'Borachio' means 'drunkard' in Spanish.

99 **dear**: 1 expensive; 2 fine

102 **will**: want / demand

104 **unconfirmed**: inexperienced
105–6 **the fashion … man**: i.e. clothes don't make the man

111 **deformed … is**: i.e. people spend a fortune trying to keep up with changing fashions
112 **Deformed**: He misunderstands, thinking it is a man's name.

116 **vane**: weather-vane

120 **reechy**: dirty
121 **Bel**: Baal (an ancient god)

THINK ABOUT for GCSE

Language

• 'Borachio' comes from the word *borracho*, which means 'drunkard' in Spanish. What is there in his manner of speaking that suggests he might be drunk?

CONRADE	I will owe thee an answer for that. And now forward with thy tale.	
BORACHIO	Stand thee close then under this pent-house, for it drizzles rain; and I will, like a true drunkard, utter all to thee.	95
WATCHMAN 2	(*Aside*) Some treason, masters: yet stand close.	
BORACHIO	... Therefore know I have earned of Don John a thousand ducats.	
CONRADE	Is it possible that any villainy should be so dear?	
BORACHIO	Thou should'st rather ask if it were possible any villainy should be so rich – for when rich villains have need of poor ones, poor ones may make what price they will.	100
CONRADE	I wonder at it.	
BORACHIO	That shows thou art unconfirmed. Thou knowest that the fashion of a doublet, or a hat, or a cloak, is nothing to a man.	105
CONRADE	Yes, it is apparel.	
BORACHIO	I mean, the fashion.	
CONRADE	Yes, the fashion is the fashion.	
BORACHIO	Tush! I may as well say the fool's the fool. But see'st thou not what a deformed thief this fashion is?	110
WATCHMAN 1	(*Aside*) I know that Deformed. 'A has been a vile thief this seven year. 'A goes up and down like a gentleman. I remember his name.	
BORACHIO	Didst thou not hear somebody?	115
CONRADE	No; 'twas the vane on the house.	
BORACHIO	See'st thou not, I say, what a deformed thief this fashion is, how giddily 'a turns about all the hot bloods between fourteen and five-and-thirty – some times fashioning them like Pharaoh's soldiers in the reechy painting, sometime like god Bel's priests in the old church-	120

Borachio explains how he has tricked Claudio and Don Pedro into believing that Hero is unfaithful. The watchmen jump out and arrest Borachio and Conrade.

THINK ABOUT for GCSE

Structure and form

- We are only ever given a report of the scene intended to convince Claudio and Don Pedro that Hero had a man in her room. In some productions a scene is added in which we actually see it acted out. What are the advantages and disadvantages of inserting such a scene?

Language

- The watchman claims to have 'recovered the most dangerous piece of lechery' (line 151). He presumably means that he has uncovered treachery – but in what way is his malapropism (use of the wrong word) oddly appropriate?

123 **smirched**: dirty
cod-piece: A fabric pouch attached to the front of the breeches.
124 **massy**: enormous

135 **possessed**: given information
136 **amiable**: loving

140 **oaths**: sworn promises

146 **o'ernight**: last night

151 **recovered**: He means 'discovered'.
lechery: sexual wickedness (he means 'treachery')
154 **lock**: long lock of hair

	window, sometime like the shaven Hercules in the smirched worm-eaten tapestry, where his cod-piece seems as massy as his club?
CONRADE	All this I see. And I see that the fashion wears out more apparel than the man. But art not thou thyself giddy with the fashion too, that thou hast shifted out of thy tale into telling me of the fashion?
BORACHIO	Not so, neither. But know that I have tonight wooed Margaret, the Lady Hero's gentlewoman, by the name of Hero. She leans me out at her mistress' chamber-window, bids me a thousand times goodnight – I tell this tale vilely – I should first tell thee how the Prince, Claudio, and my master, planted, and placed, and possessed, by my master Don John, saw afar off in the orchard this amiable encounter.
CONRADE	And thought they Margaret was Hero?
BORACHIO	Two of them did, the Prince and Claudio – but the devil my master knew she was Margaret. And partly by his oaths, which first possessed them, partly by the dark night, which did deceive them, but chiefly by my villainy, which did confirm any slander that Don John had made, away went Claudio enraged: swore he would meet her, as he was appointed, next morning at the temple, and there, before the whole congregation, shame her with what he saw o'ernight, and send her home again without a husband.
WATCHMAN 1	(*Coming forward*) We charge you, in the Prince's name, stand!
WATCHMAN 2	Call up the right Master Constable. We have here recovered the most dangerous piece of lechery that ever was known in the commonwealth.
WATCHMAN 1	And one Deformed is one of them: I know him, 'a wears a lock.

125

130

135

140

145

150

Borachio and Conrade are led off to prison by the Watch.

158   **obey**: He means 'order'.

160   **goodly commodity**: fine goods
160–1 **taken … bills**: 1 arrested by these men's weapons; 2 bought on credit in exchange for bonds
162   **in question**: 1 dubious; 2 much sought after

THINK ABOUT *for* GCSE

Themes and issues

- In what ways has this scene contributed to the theme of **noting and misunderstanding**?

Language

- Borachio and Conrade exchange word-play at the end of this scene, in lines 160 to 163. What is its effect as they are led away?

| CONRADE | Masters, masters – | 155 |

WATCHMAN 2 You'll be made bring Deformed forth, I warrant you.

CONRADE Masters –

WATCHMAN 1 Never speak, we charge you. Let us obey you to go with us.

BORACHIO We are like to prove a goodly commodity, being taken 160 up of these men's bills.

CONRADE A commodity in question, I warrant you. (*To the* WATCHMEN) Come, we'll obey you.

Exeunt.

Act 3 Scene 4

In this scene ...

- Margaret helps Hero to prepare for the wedding.
- Beatrice arrives behaving miserably and claiming to have a cold.
- Margaret and Hero mock Beatrice for being love-sick.

Margaret is helping Hero to prepare for the wedding.

THINK ABOUT
***for* GCSE**

Language

- What is the effect of the references in this scene and in Act 3 Scene 2 about dress and fashion? Which theme might it contribute to?

Structure and form

- What makes Hero say that her heart is 'exceeding heavy' (lines 22 to 23)? What effect does her mood have on our predictions about what will happen to her?

6   **Troth**: In truth
   rebato: A wired collar supporting a lace ruff.

12   **tire**: head-dress

16   **exceeds**: is better than all others
17   **in respect of**: compared with
18   **cuts**: ornamental slashes in the fabric
   laced with silver: decorated with silver lace
19   **down-sleeves**: tight long sleeves
   side-sleeves: ornamental long sleeves hanging from the shoulders
19–20   **round ... tinsel**: lined with silvery-blue fabric
20   **quaint**: elegant
21   **on't**: of it
25   **Fie upon thee**: Shame on you

Inside Leonato's house.

Enter HERO, MARGARET, *and* URSULA.

HERO	Good Ursula, wake my cousin Beatrice, and desire her to rise.
URSULA	I will, lady.
HERO	And bid her come hither.
URSULA	Well. 5

Exit.

MARGARET	Troth, I think your other rebato were better.
HERO	No, pray thee, good Meg, I'll wear this.
MARGARET	By my troth, 's not so good, and I warrant your cousin will say so.
HERO	My cousin's a fool and thou art another. I'll wear none 10 but this.
MARGARET	I like the new tire within excellently, if the hair were a thought browner. And your gown's a most rare fashion, i'faith. I saw the Duchess of Milan's gown that they praise so. 15
HERO	O, that exceeds, they say.
MARGARET	By my troth, 's but a nightgown in respect of yours – cloth o' gold, and cuts, and laced with silver, set with pearls, down-sleeves, side-sleeves, and skirts round underborne with a bluish tinsel. But for a fine, quaint, 20 graceful and excellent fashion, yours is worth ten on't.
HERO	God give me joy to wear it, for my heart is exceeding heavy.
MARGARET	'Twill be heavier soon, by the weight of a man.
HERO	Fie upon thee! Art not ashamed? 25

Beatrice claims to be miserable because she has a head-cold.

29 saving your reverence: begging your pardon
An: If
bad: bawdy / dirty
30 wrest true speaking: distort the meaning of honest words
33 light: immoral

35 coz: cousin

39 Clap's into: Let's sing
Light o'Love: a popular dance tune
burden: 1 bass harmony; 2 weight of a man
41 light o'love: a loose woman
with your heels: 'Light heels' was slang for an unchaste woman.
42 barnes: barns (with word-play on 'bairns' – children)
45–6 Heigh-ho! … husband?: 'Heigh-ho' could be a hunting-call as well as a sighing sound.
47 H: The letter 'H' sounded like the word 'ache'.
48 an … Turk: if you haven't changed your beliefs
48–9 there's … star: i.e. you can't be certain of anything any more
50 trow: do you think

54 am stuffed: have a head-cold
55 and stuffed: i.e. having had sex, or pregnant

THINK ABOUT for GCSE

Structure and form

• The word 'stuffed', used in lines 54 and 55, clearly has a sexual meaning and Margaret's reply is intended as a joke. But what do we know about the plot which gives the joke a serious edge?

MARGARET	Of what, lady? Of speaking honourably? Is not marriage honourable in a beggar? Is not your lord honourable without marriage? I think you would have me say, 'saving your reverence, a husband'. An bad thinking do not wrest true speaking, I'll offend nobody. Is there any harm in 'the heavier for a husband'? None, I think, an it be the right husband and the right wife. Otherwise 'tis light, and not heavy. Ask my Lady Beatrice else: here she comes.

Enter BEATRICE.

HERO	Good morrow, coz.	35
BEATRICE	Good morrow, sweet Hero.	
HERO	Why, how now? Do you speak in the sick tune?	
BEATRICE	I am out of all other tune, methinks.	
MARGARET	Clap's into 'Light o'Love': that goes without a burden. Do you sing it, and I'll dance it.	40
BEATRICE	Ye light o'love with your heels! Then if your husband have stables enough, you'll see he shall lack no barnes.	
MARGARET	O illegitimate construction! I scorn that with my heels.	
BEATRICE	'Tis almost five o'clock, cousin: 'tis time you were ready. By my troth, I am exceeding ill. Heigh-ho!	45
MARGARET	For a hawk, a horse, or a husband?	
BEATRICE	For the letter that begins them all, H.	
MARGARET	Well, an you be not turned Turk, there's no more sailing by the star.	
BEATRICE	What means the fool, trow?	50
MARGARET	Nothing I: but God send everyone their heart's desire!	
HERO	These gloves the Count sent me: they are an excellent perfume.	
BEATRICE	I am stuffed, cousin; I cannot smell.	
MARGARET	A maid, and stuffed! There's goodly catching of cold.	55

Margaret teases Beatrice for being love-sick. The women rush off to finish dressing for the wedding.

57   **apprehension**: wit

59   **rarely**: excellently

62   **Carduus Benedictus**: A medicinal herb.
63   **qualm**: sickness

65   **moral**: hidden meaning

70   **list**: please

76   **eats … grudging**: has an appetite and doesn't complain

80   **Not a false gallop**: i.e. I am speaking the truth.

THINK ABOUT for GCSE

Language

- How does Margaret get the better of Beatrice's wit in this scene?

Characterisation

- How would you describe the different moods of Margaret, Hero and Beatrice here?

BEATRICE	O, God help me! God help me! How long have you professed apprehension?
MARGARET	Ever since you left it. Doth not my wit become me rarely?
BEATRICE	It is not seen enough. You should wear it in your cap. 60 By my troth, I am sick.
MARGARET	Get you some of this distilled Carduus Benedictus, and lay it to your heart. It is the only thing for a qualm.
HERO	There thou prick'st her with a thistle.
BEATRICE	Benedictus! Why Benedictus? You have some moral in 65 this 'Benedictus'?
MARGARET	Moral? No, by my troth, I have no moral meaning: I meant plain holy-thistle. You may think perchance that I think you are in love. Nay, by'r Lady, I am not such a fool to think what I list, nor I list not to think what I can 70 – nor indeed I cannot think, if I would think my heart out of thinking, that you are in love, or that you will be in love, or that you can be in love. Yet Benedick was such another, and now is he become a man. He swore he would never marry, and yet now, in despite of his 75 heart, he eats his meat without grudging. And how you may be converted I know not; but methinks you look with your eyes as other women do.
BEATRICE	What pace is this that thy tongue keeps?
MARGARET	Not a false gallop. 80

Enter URSULA.

URSULA	Madam, withdraw. The Prince, the Count, Signior Benedick, Don John and all the gallants of the town are come, to fetch you to church.
HERO	Help to dress me, good coz, good Meg, good Ursula.

Exeunt.

ACT 3. SCENE 5

In this scene ...

- Dogberry and Verges visit Leonato to tell him about the arrest of Borachio and Conrade.
- Leonato receives their confused report, but is in too much of a hurry to investigate further.

Dogberry and Verges report to Leonato with important news. Dogberry's difficulty with words and self-importance prevent him from delivering his message.

2–3 confidence ... decerns: He means 'conference' ... 'concerns'.

3 nearly: closely

8 Goodman: A title used of middle-class men.

9 blunt: He means 'sharp'.

14 odorous: He means 'odious' (hateful).
palabras: few words (from Spanish)

THINK ABOUT for GCSE

Language

- Dogberry clearly misunderstands Leonato's complaint that he is 'tedious' (line 15) and takes it as a compliment. Looking at his response (in lines 16 to 24) what does he appear to think it means?

Performance and staging

- How can Dogberry's misunderstanding be used for comic effect in performance?

22 exclamation: He means 'acclamation' (praise).

26 fain: like to

At Leonato's house.

Enter LEONATO, *with Constable* DOGBERRY, *and* VERGES.

LEONATO	What would you with me, honest neighbour?
DOGBERRY	Marry, sir, I would have some confidence with you that decerns you nearly.
LEONATO	Brief, I pray you – for you see it is a busy time with me.
DOGBERRY	Marry, this it is, sir.
VERGES	Yes, in truth it is, sir.
LEONATO	What is it, my good friends?
DOGBERRY	Goodman Verges, sir, speaks a little off the matter – an old man, sir, and his wits are not so blunt as, God help, I would desire they were – but, in faith, honest as the skin between his brows.
VERGES	Yes, I thank God I am as honest as any man living that is an old man and no honester than I.
DOGBERRY	Comparisons are odorous – palabras, neighbour Verges.
LEONATO	Neighbours, you are tedious.
DOGBERRY	It pleases your worship to say so, but we are the poor Duke's officers. But truly, for mine own part, if I were as tedious as a king, I could find it in my heart to bestow it all of your worship.
LEONATO	All thy tediousness on me, ah?
DOGBERRY	Yea, an 'twere a thousand pound more than 'tis, for I hear as good exclamation on your worship as of any man in the city. And though I be but a poor man, I am glad to hear it.
VERGES	And so am I.
LEONATO	I would fain know what you have to say.

5

10

15

20

25

Leonato has no time to spare. He asks Dogberry to question the prisoners himself.

28 **ta'en**: arrested
    arrant knaves: complete villains

37 **he ... you**: he's not in your class

41 **comprehended ... aspicious**: He means 'apprehended' ... 'suspicious'.

45 **suffigance**: He means 'sufficient'.

47 **stay**: are waiting

49 **wait upon**: come to

55–6 **to a non-come**: out of their wits / bewildered

57 **excommunication**: He means 'examination'.

THINK ABOUT for GCSE

Structure and form

• In lines 27 to 29, Verges comes close to giving Leonato the news that would avert disaster. How does this build the dramatic tension?

• Dogberry, Verges and the Watch did not appear until Act 3 Scene 3. What purposes have they served in the play so far?

Characterisation

• What kind of character is Dogberry? Think about what causes him to interrupt Verges in lines 30 to 36.

VERGES	Marry, sir, our watch tonight, excepting your worship's presence, ha' ta'en a couple of as arrant knaves as any in Messina.

DOGBERRY A good old man, sir, he will be talking. As they say, 30
'When the age is in, the wit is out'. God help us, it is a
world to see! Well said, i'faith, neighbour Verges; well,
God's a good man. An two men ride of a horse, one
must ride behind. An honest soul, i' faith, sir, by my troth
he is, as ever broke bread. But God is to be worshipped. 35
All men are not alike. Alas, good neighbour!

LEONATO Indeed, neighbour, he comes too short of you.

DOGBERRY Gifts that God gives.

LEONATO I must leave you.

DOGBERRY One word, sir. Our watch, sir, have indeed 40
comprehended two aspicious persons, and we would
have them this morning examined before your worship.

LEONATO Take their examination yourself and bring it me. I am
now in great haste, as it may appear unto you.

DOGBERRY It shall be suffigance. 45

LEONATO Drink some wine ere you go. Fare you well!

Enter a MESSENGER.

MESSENGER My lord, they stay for you to give your daughter to her
husband.

LEONATO I'll wait upon them: I am ready.

Exit LEONATO, *with* MESSENGER.

DOGBERRY Go good partner, go, get you to Francis Seacoal. Bid 50
him bring his pen and inkhorn to the jail. We are now
to examination these men.

VERGES And we must do it wisely.

DOGBERRY We will spare for no wit, I warrant you. (*Pointing to
his head*) Here's that shall drive some of them to a 55
non-come. Only get the learnèd writer to set down our
excommunication, and meet me at the jail.

Exeunt.

In this scene ...

- At the wedding Claudio claims that Hero is not a virgin.
- Hero faints. Leonato is furious at his daughter.
- The Friar does not believe that Hero is guilty. He suggests that they pretend she has died to make Claudio feel sorry.
- Beatrice and Benedick reveal their true feelings for one another.
- Benedick agrees to challenge Claudio to a duel.

Everyone assembles at the church to witness the wedding of Claudio and Hero. The service begins.

1   **plain form**: essentials

10   **conjoined**: united

THINK ABOUT for GCSE

Characterisation

- What mood is Leonato in as the scene opens? At what point does his mood begin to change and why?

Performance and staging

- Why might it be better for the staging of the play only to have 'the plain form' in this scene, rather than the complete marriage service?

18–19   **Interjections ... he!**: Benedick's joke refers to grammar textbooks, where interjections or interruptions were listed according to the emotions expressed, e.g. laughing.

20   **thee by**: aside
by your leave: I beg your pardon

21   **unconstrainèd**: free / unforced

25   **counterpoise**: balance

116

In the church.

Enter DON PEDRO, DON JOHN, LEONATO, FRIAR FRANCIS, CLAUDIO, BENEDICK, HERO, BEATRICE *and* ATTENDANTS.

LEONATO	Come, Friar Francis, be brief: only to the plain form of marriage, and you shall recount their particular duties afterwards.
FRIAR	You come hither, my lord, to marry this lady?
CLAUDIO	No.
LEONATO	To be married *to* her, Friar! You come to marry her.
FRIAR	Lady, you come hither to be married to this Count?
HERO	I do.
FRIAR	If either of you know any inward impediment why you should not be conjoined, I charge you on your souls to utter it.
CLAUDIO	Know you any, Hero?
HERO	None, my lord.
FRIAR	Know you any, Count?
LEONATO	I dare make his answer: none.
CLAUDIO	O what men dare do! What men may do! What men daily do, not knowing what they do!
BENEDICK	How now! Interjections? Why, then, some be of laughing, as *ah, ha, he!*
CLAUDIO	Stand thee by, Friar. Father, by your leave: Will you with free and unconstrainèd soul Give me this maid, your daughter?
LEONATO	As freely, son, as God did give her me.
CLAUDIO	And what have I to give you back, whose worth May counterpoise this rich and precious gift?

5

10

15

20

25

Claudio harshly announces that he will not marry Hero because she is not a virgin. Hero is bewildered and Leonato demands an explanation.

26 render: return

27 learn: teach

31 maid: virgin

35 To witness: as proof of

38 luxurious: lustful

41 approvèd wanton: proven whore

42 proof: test or trial of Hero

45 known: had sex with

47 extenuate: excuse

49 large: suggestive

51 comely: appropriate

53 Out … Seeming: Curse you for seeming innocent
write against it: speak out against this kind of pretence

54 Dian: Diana, goddess of the moon and chastity

55 be blown: comes into bloom

57 Venus: the goddess of love and sex

59 wide: wildly / wide of the mark

THINK ABOUT for GCSE

Themes and issues

• **Deception and disguise**: In lines 32 to 33, Claudio describes Don John without realising it. Which other lines in this scene refer to appearance giving a misleading version of reality?

DON PEDRO	Nothing, unless you render her again.
CLAUDIO	Sweet Prince, you learn me noble thankfulness.
	There, Leonato, take her back again:
	Give not this rotten orange to your friend.
	She's but the sign and semblance of her honour.
	Behold how like a maid she blushes here!
	O, what authority and show of truth
	Can cunning sin cover itself withal!
	Comes not that blood as modest evidence
	To witness simple virtue? Would you not swear,
	All you that see her, that she were a maid
	By these exterior shows? But she is none.
	She knows the heat of a luxurious bed.
	Her blush is guiltiness, not modesty.
LEONATO	What do you mean, my lord?
CLAUDIO	Not to be married;
	Not to knit my soul to an approvèd wanton.
LEONATO	Dear my lord, if you in your own proof
	Have vanquished the resistance of her youth,
	And made defeat of her virginity –
CLAUDIO	I know what you would say. If I have known her,
	You will say she did embrace me as a husband,
	And so extenuate the 'forehand sin.
	No, Leonato,
	I never tempted her with word too large,
	But, as a brother to his sister, showed
	Bashful sincerity and comely love.
HERO	And seemed I ever otherwise to you?
CLAUDIO	Out on thee! Seeming! I will write against it.
	You seem to me as Dian in her orb,
	As chaste as is the bud ere it be blown.
	But you are more intemperate in your blood
	Than Venus, or those pampered animals
	That rage in savage sensuality.
HERO	Is my lord well, that he doth speak so wide?
LEONATO	Sweet Prince, why speak not you?

Line numbers: 30, 35, 40, 45, 50, 55

119

Don Pedro supports Claudio's slander, saying that they saw Hero speak to a man at her window the previous night.

THINK ABOUT for GCSE

Characterisation

- Don Pedro has said very little so far. What do lines 60 to 62 reveal about the source of his feelings?

- Hero is accused of 'talking' with a man 'at her chamber-window' (line 88). Have you formed an impression of Hero as a 'talkative' or a 'silent' character, compared with the other women? Look back at Act 2 Scene 1, lines 43 to 48 and lines 57 to 69, for example.

Context

- In Shakespeare's time, marriage in wealthy families could be likened to a financial transaction. Which statements suggest that Claudio regards Hero as 'property' to be owned?

- What does this scene reveal about attitudes to a woman's reputation in Shakespeare's time?

61 **gone about**: worked hard
62 **stale**: prostitute

65 **nuptial**: wedding

71 **kindly**: natural

75 **catechizing**: questioning

79 **Hero … virtue**: Hero has blotted her own name, which, in myth, stands for loyal love.

89 **liberal**: 1 coarse / foul-mouthed; 2 talkative

DON PEDRO	What should I speak? **60** I stand dishonoured, that have gone about To link my dear friend to a common stale.
LEONATO	Are these things spoken, or do I but dream?
DON JOHN	Sir, they are spoken; and these things are true.
BENEDICK	(*Aside*) This looks not like a nuptial.
HERO	True? O God! **65**
CLAUDIO	Leonato, stand I here? Is this the Prince? Is this the Prince's brother? Is this face Hero's? Are our eyes our own?
LEONATO	All this is so: but what of this, my lord?
CLAUDIO	Let me but move one question to your daughter; **70** And, by that fatherly and kindly power That you have in her, bid her answer truly.
LEONATO	I charge thee do so, as thou art my child.
HERO	O God defend me! How am I beset! What kind of catechizing call you this? **75**
CLAUDIO	To make you answer truly to your name.
HERO	Is it not Hero? Who can blot that name With any just reproach?
CLAUDIO	Marry, that can Hero. Hero itself can blot out Hero's virtue. What man was he talked with you yesternight **80** Out at your window betwixt twelve and one? Now, if you are a maid, answer to this.
HERO	I talked with no man at that hour, my lord.
DON PEDRO	Why, then are you no maiden. Leonato: I am sorry you must hear. Upon mine honour, **85** Myself, my brother, and this grievèd Count Did see her, hear her, at that hour last night, Talk with a ruffian at her chamber-window – Who hath, indeed, most like a liberal villain, Confessed the vile encounters they have had **90** A thousand times in secret.

Hero faints. Don Pedro, Don John and Claudio leave but Benedick stays to help her.

95 **misgovernment**: bad behaviour

100 **impious**: unholy
101 **For thee**: Because of you
     gates of love: i.e. heart, eyes, mind (the ways in which love might come to him)
102 **conjecture**: suspicion

106 **Wherefore**: Why

108 **Smother ... up**: i.e. cause her to faint

THINK ABOUT for GCSE

Structure and form

- What words or actions appear to be the last straw for Hero, causing her to faint (lines 105 to 106)?

Characterisation

- Look at lines 108 to 109. Why do you think Benedick stays behind rather than leaving with the other men? List the conflicting reasons he might have for (a) leaving with Don Pedro and (b) staying behind.

114 **look up**: 1 open your eyes, i.e. recover; 2 i.e. to heaven, as though she were innocent

DON JOHN	Fie, fie, they are
	Not to be named, my lord, not to be spoke of!
	There is not chastity enough in language
	Without offence to utter them. Thus, pretty lady,
	I am sorry for thy much misgovernment. 95

CLAUDIO	O Hero! What a Hero hadst thou been,
	If half thy outward graces had been placed
	About thy thoughts and counsels of thy heart!
	But fare thee well, most foul, most fair! Farewell,
	Thou pure impiety and impious purity! 100
	For thee I'll lock up all the gates of love,
	And on my eyelids shall conjecture hang,
	To turn all beauty into thoughts of harm,
	And never shall it more be gracious.

LEONATO	Hath no man's dagger here a point for me? 105

HERO faints.

BEATRICE	Why, how now, cousin! Wherefore sink you down?

DON JOHN	Come, let us go. These things, come thus to light,
	Smother her spirits up.

Exit DON PEDRO, with DON JOHN and CLAUDIO.

BENEDICK	How doth the lady?

BEATRICE	Dead, I think. Help, uncle!
	Hero! Why, Hero! Uncle! Signior Benedick! Friar! 110

LEONATO	O Fate! Take not away thy heavy hand.
	Death is the fairest cover for her shame
	That may be wished for.

HERO stirs.

BEATRICE	How now, cousin Hero?

FRIAR	Have comfort, lady.

LEONATO	Dost thou look up?

FRIAR	Yea, wherefore should she not? 115

Leonato is furious and ashamed at the accusation. He believes it because it came from Don Pedro and Claudio.

118 printed ... blood: 1 revealed by her blushes; 2 part of her nature

122 on the rearward of: immediately following

124 Chid ... frame: Did I reproach nature for giving me only one child

128 issue: child

129 smirchèd ... mired ...: dirtied ... muddied ...

132–4 But mine ... not mine: Leonato's grief and shame are mainly based on how extremely he has loved Hero and on how her disgrace reflects on him.

138 salt: Used to preserve meat to stop it rotting.

140 attired: wrapped

142 belied: slandered

143 bedfellow: Someone who shared a bed.

THINK ABOUT for GCSE

Language

• In your opinion, what is the worst thing Leonato says in his outburst at his daughter (lines 116 to 150)?

Characterisation

• In what ways might audiences' impressions of Leonato change during this scene, compared with their view of him before this scene?

LEONATO	Wherefore! Why, doth not every earthly thing
	Cry shame upon her? Could she here deny
	The story that is printed in her blood?
	Do not live, Hero, do not ope thine eyes:
	For, did I think thou would'st not quickly die,
	Thought I thy spirits were stronger than thy shames,
	Myself would, on the rearward of reproaches,
	Strike at thy life. Grieved I, I had but one?
	Chid I for that at frugal Nature's frame?
	O, one too much by thee! Why had I one?
	Why ever wast thou lovely in my eyes?
	Why had I not with charitable hand
	Took up a beggar's issue at my gates,
	Who, smirchèd thus and mired with infamy,
	I might have said 'No part of it is mine:
	This shame derives itself from unknown loins'?
	But mine, and mine I loved and mine I praised,
	And mine that I was proud on – mine so much
	That I myself was to myself not mine,
	Valuing of her – why, she, O, she is fallen
	Into a pit of ink, that the wide sea
	Hath drops too few to wash her clean again,
	And salt too little which may season give
	To her foul tainted flesh!

120

125

130

135

BENEDICK	Sir, sir, be patient.
	For my part, I am so attired in wonder,
	I know not what to say.

140

BEATRICE	O, on my soul, my cousin is belied!

BENEDICK	Lady, were you her bedfellow last night?

BEATRICE	No, truly not – although, until last night,
	I have this twelvemonth been her bedfellow.

145

LEONATO	Confirmed, confirmed! O, that is stronger made
	Which was before barred up with ribs of iron!
	Would the two Princes lie, and Claudio lie,
	Who loved her so, that, speaking of her foulness,
	Washed it with tears? Hence from her: let her die!

150

The Friar stands up for Hero and tries to get at the truth. Benedick begins to suspect Don John of some sort of villainous trick.

155 **apparitions**: appearances

162–3 **Which ... book**: i.e. my experience and learning back up my observation
164 **divinity**: status as a holy man

169 **perjury**: lying under oath

171 **That ... nakedness**: i.e. Hero's unfaithfulness, which has been clearly exposed

175 **warrant**: allow

THINK ABOUT *for* **GCSE**

Language

• Often when people have powerful emotions to express in Shakespeare's plays, they use simple words. Look at lines 166 to 168 ('Friar, it ... damnation'). How does the fact that the last word is the only long one make it sound even worse?

178 **unmeet**: improper / inappropriate
179 **Maintained ... words**: talked

181 **misprision**: misunderstanding

182 **have ... honour**: are absolutely honourable
184 **practice**: plotting
185 **in frame of**: devising

Friar	Hear me a little.
	For I have only silent been so long,
	And given way unto this course of fortune
	By noting of the lady. I have marked
	A thousand blushing apparitions 155
	To start into her face, a thousand innocent shames
	In angel whiteness beat away those blushes.
	And in her eye there hath appeared a fire,
	To burn the errors that these Princes hold
	Against her maiden truth. Call me a fool; 160
	Trust not my reading nor my observations,
	Which with experimental seal doth warrant
	The tenor of my book; trust not my age,
	My reverence, calling, nor divinity,
	If this sweet lady lie not guiltless here 165
	Under some biting error.
Leonato	Friar, it cannot be.
	Thou see'st that all the grace that she hath left
	Is that she will not add to her damnation
	A sin of perjury: she not denies it.
	Why seek'st thou then to cover with excuse 170
	That which appears in proper nakedness?
Friar	Lady, what man is he you are accused of?
Hero	They know that do accuse me. I know none.
	If I know more of any man alive
	Than that which maiden modesty doth warrant, 175
	Let all my sins lack mercy! O my father,
	Prove you that any man with me conversed
	At hours unmeet, or that I yesternight
	Maintained the change of words with any creature,
	Refuse me, hate me, torture me to death! 180
Friar	There is some strange misprision in the Princes.
Benedick	Two of them have the very bent of honour;
	And if their wisdoms be misled in this,
	The practice of it lives in John the bastard,
	Whose spirits toil in frame of villainies. 185

The Friar advises them to pretend that Hero has died. The aim is to win sympathy for Hero, and to make Claudio feel sorry.

190 **eat**: eaten
     invention: intelligence
192 **reft**: deprived
193 **in such a kind**: to such a degree

196 **quit ... throughly**: pay them back completely

201 **mourning ostentation**: formal show of grief

THINK ABOUT
for GCSE

Relationships

• What does this scene reveal about the relationship between Leonato and Hero?

Performance and staging

• If you were the director, how would you ask Leonato and Hero to act towards one another throughout the scene? Think about the way Leonato has treated Hero in earlier scenes and in this scene.

209 **on ... birth**: look for something better to come out of this

213 **falls out**: happens
214 **prize ... worth**: do not appreciate its real value
216 **rack**: exaggerate

221 **study of imagination**: brooding thoughts
222 **organ**: aspect
223 **habit**: clothing

LEONATO	I know not. If they speak but truth of her,
	These hands shall tear her. If they wrong her honour,
	The proudest of them shall well hear of it.
	Time hath not yet so dried this blood of mine,
	Nor age so eat up my invention, 190
	Nor fortune made such havoc of my means,
	Nor my bad life reft me so much of friends,
	But they shall find, awaked in such a kind,
	Both strength of limb and policy of mind,
	Ability in means and choice of friends 195
	To quit me of them throughly.

FRIAR	Pause awhile,
	And let my counsel sway you in this case.
	Your daughter here the Princes left for dead.
	Let her awhile be secretly kept in,
	And publish it that she is dead indeed. 200
	Maintain a mourning ostentation;
	And on your family's old monument
	Hang mournful epitaphs, and do all rites
	That appertain unto a burial.

| LEONATO | What shall become of this? What will this do? 205 |

FRIAR	Marry, this, well carried, shall on her behalf
	Change slander to remorse: that is some good.
	But not for that dream I on this strange course,
	But on this travail look for greater birth.
	She dying, as it must be so maintained, 210
	Upon the instant that she was accused,
	Shall be lamented, pitied, and excused
	Of every hearer: for it so falls out
	That what we have we prize not to the worth
	Whiles we enjoy it; but being lacked and lost, 215
	Why, then we rack the value, then we find
	The virtue that possession would not show us
	Whiles it was ours. So will it fare with Claudio.
	When he shall hear she died upon his words,
	Th' idea of her life shall sweetly creep 220
	Into his study of imagination.
	And every lovely organ of her life
	Shall come apparelled in more precious habit,

Everyone agrees to the Friar's plan. Beatrice and Benedick are left alone for the first time since they discovered their love for one another.

227 **interest in**: claim to
liver: Supposedly the origin of love.

230 **doubt**: fear

233 **all ... false**: all the rest of my plan fails

236 **sort**: turns out

238 **some ... life**: i.e. in a nunnery

241 **inwardness**: close friendship

THINK ABOUT for **GCSE**

Characterisation

• How does the Friar assume that Claudio will take the news of Hero's death? From what you know of Claudio, is the Friar right in his prediction?

Themes and issues

• **Men and women**: What do you think of the Friar's 'plan B' (see lines 236 to 239)? How do you interpret the fact that the Friar does not ask Hero's opinion of his proposed plan?

245 **Being ... grief**: Since I am overwhelmed by grief

248 **to ... cure**: desperate diseases need desperate remedies
250 **prolonged**: postponed

More moving, delicate, and full of life,
Into the eye and prospect of his soul,   225
Than when she lived indeed. Then shall he mourn,
If ever love had interest in his liver,
And wish he had not so accusèd her –
No, though he thought his accusation true.
Let this be so, and doubt not but success   230
Will fashion the event in better shape
Than I can lay it down in likelihood.
But if all aim but this be levelled false,
The supposition of the lady's death
Will quench the wonder of her infamy.   235
And if it sort not well, you may conceal her,
As best befits her wounded reputation,
In some reclusive and religious life,
Out of all eyes, tongues, minds, and injuries.

BENEDICK   Signior Leonato, let the Friar advise you.   240
And though you know my inwardness and love
Is very much unto the Prince and Claudio,
Yet, by mine honour, I will deal in this
As secretly and justly as your soul
Should with your body.

LEONATO   Being that I flow in grief,   245
The smallest twine may lead me.

FRIAR   'Tis well consented. Presently away:
For to strange sores strangely they strain the cure.
Come, lady, die to live. This wedding-day
Perhaps is but prolonged: have patience and endure.   250

All exit except BENEDICK *and* BEATRICE.

BENEDICK   Lady Beatrice, have you wept all this while?

BEATRICE   Yea, and I will weep a while longer.

BENEDICK   I will not desire that.

BEATRICE   You have no reason: I do it freely.

BENEDICK   Surely I do believe your fair cousin is wronged.   255

BEATRICE   Ah, how much might the man deserve of me that would
            right her!

Beatrice and Benedick declare their love for each other. She asks him to kill Claudio for what he has done to Hero, but he refuses at first.

259 even: clear
no such friend: I have no such friend

261 office: job

THINK ABOUT for GCSE

Context

- Beatrice tells Benedick that getting revenge for Hero's shaming is 'a man's office, but not yours' (line 261). Why might she feel that Benedick is not the man to fight Claudio?

Performance and staging

- 'Kill Claudio' often gets a laugh, though Beatrice is completely serious. In a recent production, Beatrice and Benedick looked at the audience, startled that they were laughing. Why might the audience laugh? Is this an appropriate response?

Structure and form

- What possibilities does Beatrice's 'Kill Claudio' open up for the ways in which the play might end?

269 and eat it: and then have to eat your words (i.e. go back on your promise)

273 protest: declare

277 stayed ... hour: stopped me just in time

286 Tarry: Wait a moment

BENEDICK	Is there any way to show such friendship?
BEATRICE	A very even way, but no such friend.
BENEDICK	May a man do it? **260**
BEATRICE	It is a man's office, but not yours.
BENEDICK	I do love nothing in the world so well as you. Is not that strange?
BEATRICE	As strange as the thing I know not. It were as possible for me to say I loved nothing so well as you. But believe **265** me not, and yet I lie not: I confess nothing, nor I deny nothing. I am sorry for my cousin.
BENEDICK	By my sword, Beatrice, thou lovest me.
BEATRICE	Do not swear and eat it.
BENEDICK	I will swear by it that you love me; and I will make him **270** eat it that says I love not you.
BEATRICE	Will you not eat your word?
BENEDICK	With no sauce that can be devised to it. I protest I love thee.
BEATRICE	Why, then, God forgive me! **275**
BENEDICK	What offence, sweet Beatrice?
BEATRICE	You have stayed me in a happy hour. I was about to protest I loved *you*.
BENEDICK	And do it with all thy heart.
BEATRICE	I love you with so much of my heart that none is left to **280** protest.
BENEDICK	Come, bid me do anything for thee.
BEATRICE	Kill Claudio.
BENEDICK	Ha! Not for the wide world.
BEATRICE	You kill me to deny it. Farewell. **285**
BENEDICK	Tarry, sweet Beatrice.

Beatrice is furious that Claudio could get away with slandering Hero. She wishes she were a man so that she could fight Claudio herself.

295 **approved ... height**: proved in the highest degree
297 **bear ... hand**: lead her on
298 **take hands**: be joined in marriage
299 **unmitigated rancour**: bitterest hatred

302 **A proper saying**: A likely story

THINK ABOUT for GCSE

Performance and staging

• In lines 286 to 288 ('Tarry ... let me go'), Shakespeare gives the actors stage directions through the dialogue. What should they do here?

Characterisation

• At which point do you think Benedick starts to come round to the idea that he must challenge Claudio? What changes his mind?

307 **counties**: counts
308 **Comfect**: Candy

311 **curtsies**: formal, empty gestures
311–12 **only ... tongue**: all talk
312 **trim**: attractive but insincere

BEATRICE	I am gone though I am here. There is no love in you. Nay, I pray you, let me go.
BENEDICK	Beatrice –
BEATRICE	In faith, I will go.
BENEDICK	We'll be friends first.
BEATRICE	You dare easier be friends with me than fight with mine enemy.
BENEDICK	Is Claudio thine enemy?
BEATRICE	Is he not approved in the height a villain that hath slandered, scorned, dishonoured my kinswoman? O that I were a man! What, bear her in hand until they come to take hands, and then, with public accusation, uncovered slander, unmitigated rancour – O God, that I were a man! I would eat his heart in the market-place.
BENEDICK	Hear me, Beatrice –
BEATRICE	Talk with a man out at a window! A proper saying!
BENEDICK	Nay, but Beatrice –
BEATRICE	Sweet Hero! She is wronged, she is slandered, she is undone.
BENEDICK	Beat –
BEATRICE	Princes and counties! Surely, a princely testimony, a goodly count, Count Comfect – a sweet gallant, surely! O that I were a man for his sake, or that I had any friend would be a man for my sake! But manhood is melted into curtsies, valour into compliment; and men are only turned into tongue, and trim ones too. He is now as valiant as Hercules that only tells a lie and swears it. I cannot be a man with wishing: therefore I will die a woman with grieving.
BENEDICK	Tarry, good Beatrice. By this hand, I love thee.
BEATRICE	Use it for my love some other way than swearing by it.
BENEDICK	Think you in your soul the Count Claudio hath wronged Hero?

290

295

300

305

310

315

Benedick agrees to challenge
Claudio to a duel.

321 **engaged**: i.e. to fight Claudio

323 **dear**: costly, i.e. Claudio is going to
have to pay for this

THINK ABOUT for GCSE

Performance and staging

- When Benedick says 'By this hand...' (line 322), whose hand is he swearing by? What might the actor do here?

Characterisation

- How is this oath different from 'By my sword' (line 268)? What does the difference reveal about Benedick's changing feelings and attitudes?

Context

- What has this exchange between Beatrice and Benedick (lines 251 to 325) added to your understanding of the position of women in the world of the play?

Relationships

- In what ways has this scene brought Beatrice and Benedick closer together?

BEATRICE	Yea, as sure as I have a thought or a soul.

320

BENEDICK	Enough: I am engaged. I will challenge him. I will kiss your hand, and so I leave you. By this hand, Claudio shall render me a dear account. As you hear of me, so think of me. Go, comfort your cousin: I must say she is dead; and so, farewell.

325

Exeunt.

ACT 4 SCENE 2

In this scene ...

- The Sexton questions Borachio and Conrade.
- The watchmen reveal what they know about Don John's plans to shame Hero.
- The Sexton announces that Don John has fled and that Hero has died.

Dogberry and Verges bring Borachio and Conrade before the Sexton for questioning.

s.d. **gowns**: i.e. magistrates' robes

1 **dissembly**: He means 'assembly'.

2 **Sexton**: a church official

3 **malefactors**: wrong-doers

5 **exhibition**: He means 'commission' (official order).

11 **sirrah**: A form of address to social inferiors.

THINK ABOUT for GCSE

Context

- Why does Conrade need to inform Dogberry 'I am a gentleman, sir' before he gives his name in line 12? Think about Dogberry's use of 'sirrah' in line 11.

Structure and form

- What do we expect to happen when we see Dogberry taking charge of the questioning of Borachio and Conrade?

17 **defend**: forbid

23 **go about with**: outsmart

A prison.

Enter DOGBERRY, VERGES *and the* SEXTON *in gowns; and men of the Watch, with* CONRADE *and* BORACHIO.

DOGBERRY	Is our whole dissembly appeared?
VERGES	O, a stool and a cushion for the Sexton.
SEXTON	Which be the malefactors?
DOGBERRY	Marry, that am I and my partner.
VERGES	Nay, that's certain. We have the exhibition to examine. 5
SEXTON	But which are the offenders that are to be examined? Let them come before Master Constable.
DOGBERRY	Yea, marry, let them come before me. What is your name, friend?
BORACHIO	Borachio. 10
DOGBERRY	Pray, write down 'Borachio'. Yours, sirrah?
CONRADE	I am a gentleman, sir, and my name is Conrade.
DOGBERRY	Write down 'Master Gentleman Conrade'. Masters, do you serve God?
CONRADE AND BORACHIO	Yea, sir, we hope. 15
DOGBERRY	Write down that they hope they serve God – and write 'God' first, for God defend but God should go before such villains! Masters, it is proved already that you are little better than false knaves, and it will go near to be thought so shortly. How answer you for yourselves? 20
CONRADE	Marry, sir, we say we are none.
DOGBERRY	(*To the* SEXTON *and* VERGES) A marvellous witty fellow, I assure you. But I will go about with him. (*To* BORACHIO) Come you hither, sirrah: a word in your ear. Sir, I say to you, it is thought you are false knaves. 25

The watchmen speak up and give the Sexton the important details of Borachio's villainy.

27 in a tale: telling the same story

31 eftest: quickest / easiest

36 flat: blatant / obvious
37 perjury: lying on oath (He probably means 'slander'.)

42 Marry: By the Virgin Mary

THINK ABOUT *for* GCSE

Characterisation

• What does Dogberry get wrong in this scene? Think about (a) his language, (b) his incorrect legal procedures, and (c) the crime he believes Borachio and Conrade to have committed.

51 redemption: being saved from sin (He means 'damnation'.)

BORACHIO	Sir, I say to you we are none.
DOGBERRY	Well, stand aside. 'Fore God, they are both in a tale. Have you writ down that they are none?
SEXTON	Master Constable, you go not the way to examine. You must call forth the watch that are their accusers. 30
DOGBERRY	Yea, marry, that's the eftest way: let the watch come forth. Masters, I charge you in the Prince's name, accuse these men.
WATCHMAN 1	This man said, sir, that Don John, the Prince's brother, was a villain. 35
DOGBERRY	Write down Prince John a villain. Why, this is flat perjury, to call a Prince's brother villain.
BORACHIO	Master Constable –
DOGBERRY	Pray thee, fellow, peace. I do not like thy look, I promise thee. 40
SEXTON	What heard you him say else?
WATCHMAN 2	Marry, that he had received a thousand ducats of Don John for accusing the Lady Hero wrongfully.
DOGBERRY	Flat burglary as ever was committed.
VERGES	Yea, by mass, that it is. 45
SEXTON	What else, fellow?
WATCHMAN 1	And that Count Claudio did mean, upon his words, to disgrace Hero before the whole assembly, and not marry her.
DOGBERRY	O villain! Thou wilt be condemned into everlasting 50 redemption for this.
SEXTON	What else?
WATCHMAN 2	This is all.

The Sexton tells Borachio that Hero has died because of his actions. As Conrade and Borachio are being led away, Conrade calls Dogberry an ass.

THINK ABOUT *for* GCSE

Characterisation

- What evidence is there to support the suggestion that the Sexton is the only sensible man in Messina?

- Dogberry's final speech (lines 67 to 79) is a great comic moment, but it also reveals details about his life. What does he say which makes us feel sympathy for him and helps us to see him as a rounded human being?

Performance and staging

- How would you direct the actors playing Borachio and Conrade about how to react to the news of Hero's death? Should Borachio show some remorse, for example? (Bear in mind your decisions, and revise them if necessary, when you read Act 5 Scene 1, lines 217 to 249.)

60 opinioned: He means 'pinioned' (bound).

62 coxcomb: fool

65 naughty varlet: wicked (much stronger than modern 'naughty') rogue

67 suspect: He means 'respect'.

71 piety: He means 'impiety' (badness).

74–5 pretty ... flesh: handsome a man

76 go to: I'll have you know

SEXTON	And this is more, masters, than you can deny. Prince John is this morning secretly stolen away. Hero was in 55 this manner accused, in this very manner refused, and upon the grief of this suddenly died. Master Constable, let these men be bound, and brought to Leonato's. I will go before and show him their examination.

Exit.

DOGBERRY	Come, let them be opinioned.	60
VERGES	Let them be in the hands –	
CONRADE	Off, coxcomb!	
DOGBERRY	God's my life, where's the Sexton? Let him write down the Prince's officer coxcomb. Come, bind them. Thou naughty varlet!	65
CONRADE	Away! You are an ass, you are an ass.	
DOGBERRY	Dost thou not suspect my place? Dost thou not suspect my years? O that he were here to write me down an ass! But, masters, remember that I am an ass: though it be not written down, yet forget not that I am an 70 ass. No, thou villain, thou art full of piety, as shall be proved upon thee by good witness. I am a wise fellow, and, which is more, an officer; and, which is more, a householder; and, which is more, as pretty a piece of flesh as any is in Messina; and one that knows the law, 75 go to; and a rich fellow enough, go to; and a fellow that hath had losses; and one that hath two gowns and everything handsome about him. Bring him away. O that I had been writ down an ass!	

Exeunt.

In this scene ...

- Leonato is extremely upset that Hero has been disgraced. He and Antonio both challenge Claudio to a duel.
- Benedick enters and also challenges Claudio to a duel.
- When Dogberry and Verges arrive with their prisoners, Borachio confesses.
- Claudio begs Leonato to forgive him and agrees to marry Antonio's daughter.

Leonato is devastated. His brother Antonio tries to console him.

2 **second**: assist

3 **counsel**: advice

7 **do suit with**: are the same as

12 **strain**: strong emotion

14 **lineament**: feature
16 **sorry wag**: poor fool
    cry 'hem!': clear the throat
17 **Patch**: Bandage
17–18 **make ... candle-wasters**: drown grief by studying philosophy

THINK ABOUT *for* **GCSE**

Characterisation

- Some would say that Leonato was unforgivably harsh to Hero in the church scene (Act 4 Scene 1). Do you think the sorrow he seems to be expressing here is for Hero or for himself? How do you know?
- What are your feelings about Leonato?

24 **preceptial medicine**: helpful advice
25 **Fetter**: Bind
26 **air**: i.e. empty words
27 **office**: duty
28 **wring**: writhe with pain
29 **sufficiency**: ability
30 **moral**: full of moral advice

32 **advertisement**: good advice

In front of Leonato's house.

Enter LEONATO *and his brother* ANTONIO.

ANTONIO   If you go on thus, you will kill yourself;
And 'tis not wisdom thus to second grief
Against yourself.

LEONATO   I pray thee, cease thy counsel,
Which falls into mine ears as profitless
As water in a sieve. Give not me counsel,   5
Nor let no comforter delight mine ear
But such a one whose wrongs do suit with mine.
Bring me a father that so loved his child,
Whose joy of her is overwhelmed like mine,
And bid him speak of patience.   10
Measure his woe the length and breadth of mine,
And let it answer every strain for strain,
As thus for thus, and such a grief for such,
In every lineament, branch, shape, and form.
If such a one will smile and stroke his beard,   15
And, sorry wag, cry 'hem!' when he should groan,
Patch grief with proverbs, make misfortune drunk
With candle-wasters – bring him yet to me,
And I of him will gather patience.
But there is no such man. For, brother, men   20
Can counsel and speak comfort to that grief
Which they themselves not feel – but, tasting it,
Their counsel turns to passion, which before
Would give preceptial medicine to rage,
Fetter strong madness in a silken thread,   25
Charm ache with air and agony with words.
No, no: 'tis all men's office to speak patience
To those that wring under the load of sorrow,
But no man's virtue nor sufficiency
To be so moral when he shall endure   30
The like himself. Therefore give me no counsel:
My griefs cry louder than advertisement.

ANTONIO   Therein do men from children nothing differ.

145

Leonato accuses Claudio of villainy.

37 **writ the style of gods**: written in a god-like manner

38 **made … at**: scorned
chance and sufferance: fortune and enduring pain

42 **belied**: slandered

46 **Good-e'en**: Good afternoon (or evening)

49 **all is one**: it doesn't matter

53 **dissembler**: deceiver

55 **beshrew**: curse

57 **meant … to**: did not mean anything in moving to

THINK ABOUT
for GCSE

Language

- In line 53, Leonato addresses Claudio as 'thou' instead of 'you' (the polite form he used in Act 1 Scene 1). In other contexts it can be a sign of friendship, but how is he using it here when he addresses Claudio?

LEONATO	I pray thee, peace. I will be flesh and blood.
	For there was never yet philosopher 35
	That could endure the toothache patiently,
	However they have writ the style of gods,
	And made a push at chance and sufferance.
ANTONIO	Yet bend not all the harm upon yourself:
	Make those that do offend you suffer too. 40
LEONATO	There thou speak'st reason. Nay, I will do so.
	My soul doth tell me Hero is belied,
	And that shall Claudio know: so shall the Prince,
	And all of them that thus dishonour her.
ANTONIO	Here comes the Prince and Claudio hastily. 45

Enter DON PEDRO *and* CLAUDIO.

DON PEDRO	Good-e'en, good-e'en.
CLAUDIO	Good day to both of you.
LEONATO	Hear you, my lords!
DON PEDRO	We have some haste, Leonato.
LEONATO	Some haste, my lord! Well, fare you well, my lord.
	Are you so hasty now? Well, all is one.
DON PEDRO	Nay, do not quarrel with us, good old man. 50
ANTONIO	If he could right himself with quarrelling,
	Some of us would lie low.
CLAUDIO	Who wrongs him?
LEONATO	Marry, *thou* dost wrong me, thou dissembler, thou!
	– Nay, never lay thy hand upon thy sword:
	I fear thee not.
CLAUDIO	Marry, beshrew my hand 55
	If it should give your age such cause of fear.
	In faith, my hand meant nothing to my sword.

Leonato challenges Claudio to a duel.

THINK ABOUT for **GCSE**

Structure and form

- Do Claudio's reactions here suggest that this is the first time he has heard of Hero's death, or do you think he has already been told?

Characterisation

- What quality of Claudio's character is Leonato insulting in the expression 'his nice fence' (line 75)?

58 **fleer**: scorn
59 **dotard**: foolish old man

64 **lay ... by**: put aside my dignity (as an older man)
66 **trial of a man**: i.e. a duel

71 **framed**: i.e. caused

75 **nice fence**: clever skills at fencing
76 **lustihood**: physical fitness

78 **daff me**: brush me aside

82 **Win ... me**: Let him beat me first, then he can boast about it

84 **foining**: thrusting (a fencing term)

LEONATO	Tush, tush, man, never fleer and jest at me!
	I speak not like a dotard nor a fool,
	As under privilege of age to brag 60
	What I have done being young, or what would do
	Were I not old. Know, Claudio, to thy head,
	Thou hast so wronged mine innocent child and me
	That I am forced to lay my reverence by,
	And with grey hairs and bruise of many days 65
	Do challenge thee to trial of a man.
	I say thou hast belied mine innocent child.
	Thy slander hath gone through and through her heart,
	And she lies buried with her ancestors –
	O, in a tomb where never scandal slept, 70
	Save this of hers, framed by thy villainy!
CLAUDIO	My villainy?
LEONATO	Thine, Claudio; thine, I say.
DON PEDRO	You say not right, old man.
LEONATO	My lord, my lord,
	I'll prove it on his body if he dare,
	Despite his nice fence and his active practice, 75
	His May of youth and bloom of lustihood.
CLAUDIO	Away! I will not have to do with you.
LEONATO	Canst thou so daff me? Thou hast killed my child.
	If thou kill'st me, boy, thou shalt kill a man.
ANTONIO	He shall kill two of us, and men indeed; 80
	But that's no matter; let him kill one first.
	Win me and wear me: let him answer *me*.
	(*To* CLAUDIO) Come, follow me, boy: come, sir boy,
	come, follow me.
	Sir boy, I'll whip you from your foining fence –
	Nay, as I am a gentleman, I will. 85
LEONATO	Brother –

Antonio offers to fight Claudio
as well.

89 **answer a man**: back up their words

91 **apes**: fashionable fools
    jacks: scoundrels
    milksops: wimps
94 **scruple**: smallest bit
95 **Scambling**: Unruly
    out-facing: brazen
    fashion-monging: shallow / faddish
96 **cog**: cheat
97 **Go anticly**: Follow bizarre fashions
    show ... hideousness: put on a
    threatening appearance

103 **wake**: try

THINK ABOUT for GCSE

Performance and staging

• Don Pedro is the highest
  status character in the play.
  How should he say 'I will
  not hear you' (line 107)?
  How would you direct
  Leonato to react?

• What direction would you
  give to the actors playing
  Claudio and Don Pedro
  about how they should
  react after the departure of
  Leonato and Antonio, and
  on Benedick's arrival at
  line 110?

109 **smart**: hurt / suffer

ANTONIO	Content yourself. God knows I loved my niece;
	And she is dead, slandered to death by villains,
	That dare as well answer a man indeed
	As I dare take a serpent by the tongue. **90**
	Boys, apes, braggarts, jacks, milksops!

LEONATO   Brother Antony –

ANTONIO   Hold you content. What, man! I know them, yea,
           And what they weigh, even to the utmost scruple –
           Scambling, out-facing, fashion-monging boys, **95**
           That lie and cog and flout, deprave and slander,
           Go anticly, show outward hideousness,
           And speak off half a dozen dangerous words,
           How they might hurt their enemies, if they durst.
           And this is all. **100**

LEONATO   But brother Antony –

ANTONIO   Come, 'tis no matter;
           Do not you meddle: let me deal in this.

DON PEDRO Gentlemen both, we will not wake your patience.
           My heart is sorry for your daughter's death –
           But, on my honour, she was charged with nothing **105**
           But what was true and very full of proof.

LEONATO   My lord, my lord –

DON PEDRO   I will not hear you.

LEONATO   No?
           Come brother, away. I will be heard.

ANTONIO   And shall, or some of us will smart for it.

                                Exit LEONATO, *with* ANTONIO.

DON PEDRO See, see: here comes the man we went to seek. **110**

    Enter BENEDICK.

CLAUDIO   Now, signior, what news?

BENEDICK   Good day, my lord.

Don Pedro and Claudio try to
joke with Benedick but he treats
them coldly.

THINK ABOUT *for* GCSE

Characterisation

- As far as Don Pedro and
  Claudio are aware, Hero
  is dead, and they have just
  had an encounter with her
  grieving father and uncle.
  Many people therefore find
  their attitude to Leonato
  and Antonio offensive, both
  while they are present and
  after they have departed.
  What is your opinion?

Language

- Benedick's expression 'in
  the career' (line 133) is a
  term from jousting (a sport
  played on horseback with
  lances), meaning 'at full
  speed'. How else does the
  language he uses in lines
  119 to 124 hint that he is
  about to challenge Claudio?

- Don Pedro and Claudio
  mainly use the familiar
  'thou' (rather than the polite
  'you' form) to Benedick, as
  they are of similar status and
  have been friends (in lines
  117, 121, 123, 125 and
  130). How does
  Benedick reply?

115 **had like**: were likely

122 **high-proof**: extremely
    fain: like to

126–7 **beside their wit**: out of their minds
  127 **minstrels**: musicians (who 'draw' bows
       across their strings)

131 **care … cat**: i.e. worrying too much is
    bad for you (proverb)
132 **mettle**: spirit
133 **in the career**: at full speed

135 **staff**: lance
135–6 **staff … cross**: i.e. his lance was
       snapped

139 **how … girdle**: he'll have to put up
    with it / what he can do about it

152

DON PEDRO	Welcome, signior. You are almost come to part almost a fray.
CLAUDIO	We had like to have had our two noses snapped off with two old men without teeth.	115
DON PEDRO	Leonato and his brother. What think'st thou? Had we fought, I doubt we should have been too young for them.
BENEDICK	In a false quarrel there is no true valour. I came to seek you both.	120
CLAUDIO	We have been up and down to seek thee; for we are high-proof melancholy, and would fain have it beaten away. Wilt thou use thy wit?
BENEDICK	It is in my scabbard: shall I draw it?
DON PEDRO	Dost thou wear thy wit by thy side?	125
CLAUDIO	Never any did so, though very many have been beside their wit. I will bid thee draw, as we do the minstrels – draw to pleasure us.
DON PEDRO	As I am an honest man, he looks pale. (*To* BENEDICK) Art thou sick, or angry?	130
CLAUDIO	What, courage, man! What though care killed a cat, thou hast mettle enough in thee to kill care.
BENEDICK	Sir, I shall meet your wit in the career, an you charge it against me. I pray you choose another subject.
CLAUDIO	Nay, then, give him another staff: this last was broke cross.	135
DON PEDRO	By this light, he changes more and more. I think he be angry indeed.
CLAUDIO	If he be, he knows how to turn his girdle.
BENEDICK	Shall I speak a word in your ear?	140
CLAUDIO	God bless me from a challenge!

Don Pedro and Claudio
continue to try and joke with
Benedick. Benedick challenges
Claudio to a duel.

147 **so ... cheer**: Duelling was illegal, so
Claudio pretends that Benedick has
invited him to dinner.
149–51 **calf ... capon ... woodcock**: All
considered stupid creatures.
150 **curiously**: skilfully
151 **naught**: useless
152 **ambles well**: goes smoothly but with
no spirit

156 **gross**: coarse

158 **wise gentleman**: this is ironic
159 **hath the tongues**: is a master of
languages
160 **forswore**: took back
162 **trans-shape**: distort

164 **properest**: most handsome

THINK ABOUT
for GCSE

Performance and staging

• Don Pedro's light-hearted
remarks in lines 153 to
164 can seem out of place.
What evidence is there
that perhaps he has not
heard Benedick challenge
Claudio? Look at lines 148
and 184 to 187. How could
a director stage this?

• How might Benedick react
at this point to hearing about
Beatrice?

169–70 **God ... garden**: A reference to:
1 Benedick hiding in Act 3 Scene 1;
2 God seeing Adam in the garden of
Eden.

BENEDICK   (*Aside to* CLAUDIO) You are a villain. I jest not. I will make it good how you dare, with what you dare, and when you dare. Do me right, or I will protest your cowardice. You have killed a sweet lady, and her death shall fall **145** heavy on you. Let me hear from you.

CLAUDIO   Well, I will meet you, so I may have good cheer.

DON PEDRO   What, a feast, a feast?

CLAUDIO   I' faith, I thank him. He hath bid me to a calf's head and a capon, the which if I do not carve most curiously, say **150** my knife's naught. Shall I not find a woodcock too?

BENEDICK   Sir, your wit ambles well; it goes easily.

DON PEDRO   I'll tell thee how Beatrice praised *thy* wit the other day. I said, thou hadst a fine wit. 'True,' said she, 'a fine little one.' 'No,' said I, 'a great wit.' 'Right,' says she, 'a great **155** gross one.' 'Nay,' said I, 'a good wit.' 'Just,' said she, 'it hurts nobody.' 'Nay,' said I, 'the gentleman is wise.' 'Certain,' said she, 'a wise gentleman.' 'Nay,' said I, 'he hath the tongues.' 'That I believe,' said she, 'for he swore a thing to me on Monday night which he forswore on **160** Tuesday morning. There's a double tongue: there's two tongues.' Thus did she, an hour together, trans-shape thy particular virtues. Yet at last she concluded with a sigh, thou wast the properest man in Italy.

CLAUDIO   For the which she wept heartily, and said she cared not. **165**

DON PEDRO   Yea, that she did. But yet, for all that, and if she did not hate him deadly, she would love him dearly. The old man's daughter told us all.

CLAUDIO   All, all – and, moreover, God saw him when he was hid in the garden. **170**

DON PEDRO   But when shall we set the savage bull's horns on the sensible Benedick's head?

CLAUDIO   Yea, and text underneath: 'Here dwells Benedick, the married man'?

Claudio and Don Pedro are surprised at the change in Benedick. Dogberry and Verges bring in their prisoners, Borachio and Conrade.

176 **humour**: inclination
177 **braggarts**: boasters

182 **Lord Lack-beard**: Another reference to Claudio's youth.

189–90 **doublet and hose**: i.e. his clothes

191–2 **He ... man**: The fool may think that such a man is wise, but in fact the fool is much wiser than he is.
193 **soft you**: wait a minute
sad: serious

196 **ne'er ... balance**: never again weigh evidence in her scales

201 **Hearken after**: Enquire about

THINK ABOUT for **GCSE**

Language

• Benedick calls Claudio 'Lord Lack-beard' (line 182). What do most of the insults aimed at Claudio have in common? Look back at Beatrice's, for example (Act 4 Scene 1, lines 307 to 312) and Leonato's (Act 5 Scene 1, lines 75 to 76 and 79).

Performance and staging

• If you were the director, how would you have Don Pedro react to Benedick's parting speech?

BENEDICK	Fare you well, boy; you know my mind. I will leave 175 you now to your gossip-like humour. You break jests as braggarts do their blades, which, God be thanked, hurt not. (*To* DON PEDRO) My lord, for your many courtesies I thank you. I must discontinue your company. Your brother the bastard is fled from Messina. You have 180 among you killed a sweet and innocent lady. For my Lord Lack-beard there, he and I shall meet; and till then, peace be with him.

Exit.

DON PEDRO	He is in earnest.
CLAUDIO	In most profound earnest – and, I'll warrant you, for the 185 love of Beatrice.
DON PEDRO	And hath challenged thee.
CLAUDIO	Most sincerely.
DON PEDRO	What a pretty thing man is when he goes in his doublet and hose and leaves off his wit! 190
CLAUDIO	He is then a giant to an ape; but then is an ape a doctor to such a man.
DON PEDRO	But, soft you, let me be: pluck up, my heart, and be sad. Did he not say my brother was fled?

Enter DOGBERRY, VERGES, *and men of the Watch, with* CONRADE *and* BORACHIO *as prisoners.*

DOGBERRY	(*To* BORACHIO) Come, you, sir. If justice cannot tame 195 you, she shall ne'er weigh more reasons in her balance. Nay, an you be a cursing hypocrite once, you must be looked to.
DON PEDRO	How now, two of my brother's men bound? Borachio one! 200
CLAUDIO	Hearken after their offence, my lord.
DON PEDRO	Officers, what offence have these men done?

Borachio confesses his role in disgracing Hero. Claudio is overcome and very sorry.

206 verified unjust things: He possibly means 'testified', i.e. told lies.

THINK ABOUT
for **GCSE**

Characterisation

• Borachio has been a main player in carrying out the plot to ruin Hero's reputation. What further impression do we gain from his confession (lines 217 to 229)?

Themes and issues

• **Noting and misunderstanding**: Look at Borachio's explanation in lines 217 to 229. List some occasions in the play where people have (a) been deceived by what they see and (b) expressed the truth without realising it.

Language

• Don Pedro says 'Runs not this speech like iron through your blood?' (line 230). Where else in the play are words compared with weapons that have the power to wound? (Look at Act 1 Scene 1, lines 50 to 54 and Act 5 Scene 1, line 68.) What other powers do words have, according to this play?

---

212 division: style
213 one … suited: one idea expressed in many ways

216 cunning: clever

233 practice: doing

234 composed and framed: entirely made up

237 semblance: appearance

Dogberry	Marry, sir, they have committed false report; moreover they have spoken untruths; secondarily, they are slanders; sixth and lastly, they have belied a lady; thirdly, they 205 have verified unjust things; and to conclude, they are lying knaves.
Don Pedro	First, I ask thee what they have done; thirdly, I ask thee what's their offence; sixth and lastly, why they are committed; and to conclude, what you lay to their 210 charge.
Claudio	Rightly reasoned, and in his own division. And, by my troth, there's one meaning well suited.
Don Pedro	Who have you offended, masters, that you are thus bound to your answer? This learnèd Constable is too 215 cunning to be understood. What's your offence?
Borachio	Sweet Prince, let me go no farther to mine answer. Do you hear me, and let this Count kill me. I have deceived even your very eyes. What your wisdoms could not discover, these shallow fools have brought to light – 220 who in the night overheard me confessing to this man how Don John your brother incensed me to slander the Lady Hero; how you were brought into the orchard and saw me court Margaret in Hero's garments; how you disgraced her, when you should marry her. My villainy 225 they have upon record, which I had rather seal with my death than repeat over to my shame. The lady is dead upon mine and my master's false accusation. And briefly, I desire nothing but the reward of a villain.
Don Pedro	Runs not this speech like iron through your blood? 230
Claudio	I have drunk poison whiles he uttered it.
Don Pedro	But did my brother set thee on to this?
Borachio	Yea, and paid me richly for the practice of it.
Don Pedro	He is composed and framed of treachery, And fled he is upon this villainy. 235
Claudio	Sweet Hero, now thy image doth appear In the rare semblance that I loved it first.

Claudio and Don Pedro ask Leonato to punish them in whatever way he wishes. Leonato commands Claudio and Don Pedro to tell the people of Messina that Hero was innocent, and Claudio to compose a poem in her memory.

238 plaintiffs: He means the opposite, 'the defendants'.

239 reformed: He means 'informed'.

250 beliest: wrong

258 Impose … penance: Make me suffer any punishment
invention: imagination

263 enjoin me to: impose on me

266 Possess: Inform

268 aught: in any way

269 epitaph: Words about the dead person written on a tomb.

THINK ABOUT for GCSE

Themes and issues

- **Wrongdoing, remorse and punishment:** Compare the remorse of the three wrong-doers, Borachio, Don Pedro and Claudio. Who takes the blame? What do the others say? In particular, do you agree with Claudio's description of his own behaviour (lines 259 to 260)?

Performance and staging

- Claudio's and Don Pedro's apologies in lines 256 to 263 often seem rather thin. How would you direct the actors to say them and Leonato to respond?

DOGBERRY   Come, bring away the plaintiffs. By this time our Sexton hath reformed Signior Leonato of the matter. And, masters, do not forget to specify, when time and place 240 shall serve, that I am an ass.

VERGES   Here, here comes master Signior Leonato, and the Sexton too.

Enter LEONATO *and* ANTONIO, *with the* SEXTON.

LEONATO   Which is the villain? Let me see his eyes,
That, when I note another man like him, 245
I may avoid him. Which of these is he?

BORACHIO   If you would know your wronger, look on me.

LEONATO   Art thou the slave that with thy breath hast killed
Mine innocent child?

BORACHIO   Yea, even I alone.

LEONATO   No, not so, villain, thou beliest thyself – 250
Here stand a pair of honourable men,
A third is fled, that had a hand in it.
I thank you, Princes, for my daughter's death:
Record it with your high and worthy deeds.
'Twas bravely done, if you bethink you of it. 255

CLAUDIO   I know not how to pray your patience,
Yet I must speak. Choose your revenge yourself.
Impose me to what penance your invention
Can lay upon my sin. Yet sinned I not
But in mistaking.

DON PEDRO   By my soul, nor I. 260
And yet, to satisfy this good old man,
I would bend under any heavy weight
That he'll enjoin me to.

LEONATO   I cannot bid you bid my daughter live:
That were impossible. But I pray you both, 265
Possess the people in Messina here
How innocent she died. And if your love
Can labour aught in sad invention,
Hang her an epitaph upon her tomb

Leonato commands Claudio to marry Antonio's daughter in place of Hero. Dogberry steps in and reminds Leonato that Conrade called him an ass.

276 Give ... right: i.e. Marry her

279–80 dispose ... Claudio: i.e. from now on I put myself entirely under your guidance

282 naughty: wicked

284 packed: involved

THINK ABOUT for GCSE

Structure and form

- Leonato invents another niece. Why does he do this?

- In what ways has the function of the Watch been (a) to reassure us that all will be well; while (b) to hold back information that will make everything well?

Themes and issues

- **Wrongdoing, remorse and punishment**: How would you respond to the suggestion that Claudio is being rewarded here rather than punished?

289–90 under ... black: written down

294 borrows ... name: i.e. begs

296 lend ... sake: not give charity

300 youth: Another of Dogberry's mistakes.

301 pains: trouble

302 God ... foundation: He is thanking Leonato as though he is receiving money from a charity.

And sing it to her bones: sing it tonight. 270
Tomorrow morning come you to my house;
And since you could not be my son-in-law,
Be yet my nephew. My brother hath a daughter,
Almost the copy of my child that's dead;
And she alone is heir to both of us. 275
Give her the right you should have given her cousin,
And so dies my revenge.

CLAUDIO   O noble sir!
Your over-kindness doth wring tears from me.
I do embrace your offer – and dispose
For henceforth of poor Claudio. 280

LEONATO Tomorrow then I will expect your coming;
Tonight I take my leave. This naughty man
Shall face to face be brought to Margaret,
Who I believe was packed in all this wrong,
Hired to it by your brother.

BORACHIO   No, by my soul, she was not, 285
Nor knew not what she did when she spoke to me;
But always hath been just and virtuous
In anything that I do know by her.

DOGBERRY Moreover, sir, which indeed is not under white and
black, this plaintiff here, the offender, did call me ass. I 290
beseech you, let it be remembered in his punishment.
And also, the watch heard them talk of one Deformed:
they say he wears a key in his ear and a lock hanging
by it, and borrows money in God's name, the which he
hath used so long and never paid, that now men grow 295
hard-hearted and will lend nothing for God's sake. Pray
you, examine him upon that point.

LEONATO I thank thee for thy care and honest pains.

DOGBERRY Your worship speaks like a most thankful and reverend
youth, and I praise God for you. 300

LEONATO There's for thy pains. (*Gives him money.*)

DOGBERRY God save the foundation!

LEONATO Go; I discharge thee of thy prisoner, and I thank thee.

Dogberry leaves the prisoners with Leonato for him to punish. Leonato reminds Claudio and Don Pedro to meet the next day for Claudio's wedding.

304   arrant: total

309   prohibit it: He means the opposite, 'make it happen'.

311   look for: will expect

314   lewd: base

THINK ABOUT *for* GCSE

Characterisation

• What is your final impression of Dogberry? Do you find him merely ridiculous or have you gained some affection or even sympathy for him?

Themes and issues

• **Wrongdoing, remorse and punishment**: The scene ends with a reference to Margaret. In the Branagh film, Margaret is so guilty and frightened that she runs away from the wedding. How guilty is she, in your opinion?

DOGBERRY   I leave an arrant knave with your worship – which
             I beseech your worship to correct yourself, for the   305
             example of others. God keep your worship! I wish your
             worship well. God restore you to health! I humbly give
             you leave to depart; and if a merry meeting may be
             wished, God prohibit it! Come, neighbour.

                                          Exit DOGBERRY, *with* VERGES.

LEONATO   Until tomorrow morning, lords, farewell.   310

ANTONIO   Farewell, my lords: we look for you tomorrow.

DON PEDRO   We will not fail.

CLAUDIO   Tonight I'll mourn with Hero.

                                          Exit DON PEDRO, *with* CLAUDIO.

LEONATO   (*To the men of the Watch*)
             Bring you these fellows on. We'll talk with Margaret,
             How her acquaintance grew with this lewd fellow.

                                                              Exeunt.

In this scene ...

- Benedick tries to write a love poem for Beatrice.
- Benedick tells Beatrice that he has challenged Claudio.
- Ursula brings news of Hero's innocence and that Don John was responsible for what happened.

Benedick asks Margaret to fetch Beatrice. He tries to write a love poem.

THINK ABOUT for GCSE

Language

- The conversation between Benedick and Margaret is full of sexual innuendos (double meanings) including: 'come over' (have sex with), 'swords / pikes' and 'bucklers' (the male and female sex organs), and 'vice' (a woman's thighs). What effect does it have at this point in the play?

Characterisation

- Does Benedick's friendly conversation with Margaret make us feel more sympathetic towards her?

Context

- Benedick's song (lines 18 to 21) was well known to Shakespeare's audience. Its subject was a lover begging his mistress for pity. In a modern performance, should it seem as though Benedick is singing a familiar song, or one he is trying to compose on the spot?

4–5 **come over**: exceed

5 **comely**: fair and proper (with a play on 'come over')

7 **below stairs**: i.e. in the servants' quarters

9 **foils**: light swords

12 **bucklers**: small, round shields

14 **pikes**: central spikes in shields

22–3 **Leander ... Troilus**: Both are lovers from legend.

23 **panders**: pimps

24–6 **quondam ... verse**: one-time ladies'-men (i.e. not soldiers) who are still remembered in poetry

Leonato's garden.

Enter BENEDICK *and* MARGARET.

BENEDICK	Pray thee, sweet Mistress Margaret, deserve well at my hands by helping me to the speech of Beatrice.
MARGARET	Will you then write me a sonnet in praise of my beauty?
BENEDICK	In so high a style, Margaret, that no man living shall come over it; for, in most comely truth, thou deservest it.
MARGARET	To have no man come over me! Why, shall I always keep below stairs?
BENEDICK	Thy wit is as quick as the greyhound's mouth: it catches.
MARGARET	And yours as blunt as the fencer's foils, which hit, but hurt not.
BENEDICK	A most manly wit, Margaret: it will not hurt a woman. And so, I pray thee, call Beatrice. I give thee the bucklers.
MARGARET	Give us the swords: we have bucklers of our own.
BENEDICK	If you use them, Margaret, you must put in the pikes with a vice – and they are dangerous weapons for maids.
MARGARET	Well, I will call Beatrice to you, who I think hath legs.

Exit.

BENEDICK	And therefore will come.

    (**Sings**) 'The God of love,
              That sits above,
              And knows me, and knows me,
              How pitiful I deserve –'

I mean in singing – but in loving, Leander the good swimmer, Troilus the first employer of panders, and a whole bookful of these quondam carpet-mongers, whose names yet run smoothly in the even road of a blank verse, why, they were never so truly turned over and over as my poor self in love. Marry, I cannot show it in rhyme. I have tried. I can find out no rhyme to 'lady'

Benedick tells Beatrice that he has challenged Claudio to a duel.

29 **innocent**: childish

32 **festival terms**: poetic language

37 **that I came**: what I came for

41 **noisome**: nasty

45 **undergoes**: i.e. has accepted (and now has to show up)

46 **subscribe**: announce

49 **politic**: well-organised

53 **epithet**: expression

THINK ABOUT for GCSE

Language

• What is the tone of the banter between Beatrice and Benedick in this scene? How does it differ in tone from their earlier exchanges (especially Act 1 Scene 1 and Act 2 Scene 1)?

• What might we work out from the fact that Benedick uses the 'thou' form and Beatrice the more polite 'you' form throughout this scene?

but 'baby' – an innocent rhyme; for 'scorn', 'horn' – a
hard rhyme; for 'school', 'fool' – a babbling rhyme: **30**
very ominous endings. No, I was not born under a
rhyming planet, nor I cannot woo in festival terms.

Enter BEATRICE.

Sweet Beatrice, would'st thou come when I called thee?

BEATRICE	Yea, signior, and depart when you bid me.
BENEDICK	O, stay but till then! **35**
BEATRICE	'Then' is spoken: fare you well now. And yet, ere I go, let me go with that I came – which is, with knowing what hath passed between you and Claudio.
BENEDICK	Only foul words: and thereupon I will kiss thee.
BEATRICE	Foul words is but foul wind, and foul wind is but foul **40** breath, and foul breath is noisome: therefore I will depart unkissed.
BENEDICK	Thou hast frighted the word out of his right sense, so forcible is thy wit. But I must tell thee plainly, Claudio undergoes my challenge; and either I must shortly hear **45** from him, or I will subscribe him a coward. And I pray thee now, tell me for which of my bad parts didst thou first fall in love with me?
BEATRICE	For them all together; which maintained so politic a state of evil that they will not admit any good part to **50** intermingle with them. But for which of my good parts did you first suffer love for me?
BENEDICK	'Suffer love!' – a good epithet. I do suffer love indeed, for I love thee against my will.
BEATRICE	In spite of your heart, I think. Alas, poor heart! If you **55** spite it for my sake, I will spite it for yours: for I will never love that which my friend hates.
BENEDICK	Thou and I are too wise to woo peaceably.
BEATRICE	It appears not in this confession. There's not one wise man among twenty that will praise himself. **60**

Ursula brings news that Hero has been proved innocent.

61 **instance**: saying

62 **time … neighbours**: old days

63–4 **live … than**: have no memorial longer than

66 **Question**: A good question

clamour: tolling the funeral bell

67 **rheum**: tears

68 **Don Worm**: 'Sir Worm' – referring to the popular idea of conscience gnawing like a worm.

THINK ABOUT for GCSE

Characterisation

- Unlike most other male characters, Benedick shows real concern for Hero (lines 71 to 72). In what ways has Benedick changed since the beginning of the play?

Performance and staging

- Benedick's 'die in thy lap' (line 84) can also mean 'have sex with you'. How might Beatrice react? Is she offended, for example, or amused? Or does she simply take no notice? Consider different possibilities and the effect each one might have.

78 **old coil**: a great to-do

80 **abused**: deceived

82 **presently**: immediately

84 **die in thy lap**: Can mean 'have sex with you'.

BENEDICK	An old, an old instance, Beatrice – that lived in the time of good neighbours. If a man do not erect in this age his own tomb ere he dies, he shall live no longer in monument than the bell rings and the widow weeps.
BEATRICE	And how long is that, think you? 65
BENEDICK	Question – why, an hour in clamour and a quarter in rheum. Therefore is it most expedient for the wise, if Don Worm, his conscience, find no impediment to the contrary, to be the trumpet of his own virtues, as I am to myself. So much for praising myself, who, I myself will 70 bear witness, is praiseworthy. And now tell me, how doth your cousin?
BEATRICE	Very ill.
BENEDICK	And how do you?
BEATRICE	Very ill too. 75
BENEDICK	Serve God, love me, and mend. There will I leave you too, for here comes one in haste.

Enter URSULA.

URSULA	Madam, you must come to your uncle. Yonder's old coil at home. It is proved my Lady Hero hath been falsely accused, the Prince and Claudio mightily abused, and 80 Don John is the author of all, who is fled and gone. Will you come presently?
BEATRICE	Will you go hear this news, signior?
BENEDICK	I will live in thy heart, die in thy lap and be buried in thy eyes. And moreover, I will go with thee to thy uncle's. 85

Exeunt.

In this scene ...

- Claudio mourns at Hero's tomb.
- Claudio and Don Pedro depart to prepare for Claudio's wedding.

Claudio hangs a poem on Hero's tomb in her memory and Balthasar sings a funeral song.

5 **guerdon**: compensation

12 **goddess of the night**: Diana

THINK ABOUT *for* **GCSE**

Performance and staging

- This scene takes place at Hero's monument. It opens at night, but dawn is approaching by the end. How would you stage this?

18 **Heavily**: Mournfully

20 **utterèd**: fully expressed

The church: near Leonato's family monument.

Enter CLAUDIO, DON PEDRO, BALTHASAR *with musicians, and three or four gentlemen carrying candles, all wearing mourning clothes.*

CLAUDIO   Is this the monument of Leonato?

A GENTLEMAN   It is, my lord.

CLAUDIO   (*Reading Hero's epitaph from a scroll*)
               Done to death by slanderous tongues
                 Was the Hero that here lies.
               Death, in guerdon of her wrongs,   5
                 Gives her fame which never dies.
               So the life that died with shame
                 Lives in death with glorious fame.
               Hang thou there upon the tomb,
                            (*Hanging the scroll on the tomb*)
               Praising her when I am dumb.   10
               Now, music, sound; and sing your solemn hymn.

BALTHASAR

    Song

               Pardon, goddess of the night,
               Those that slew thy virgin knight;
               For the which, with songs of woe,
               Round about her tomb they go.   15
               Midnight, assist our moan,
               Help us to sigh and groan,
                 Heavily, heavily.
               Graves yawn and yield your dead,
               Till death be utterèd,   20
                 Heavily, heavily.

CLAUDIO   Now, unto thy bones good night.
               Yearly will I do this rite.

Don Pedro and Claudio set off to Leonato's house for the wedding.

26 **wheels of Phoebus**: i.e. the sun

29 **several**: own

30 **weeds**: clothes

32 **Hymen**: the god of marriage
 speed's: favour us

THINK ABOUT for GCSE

Language

• Apart from the songs, there is very little rhyme in this play. But, after the rhyming epitaph and song, Don Pedro and Claudio continue to speak in rhyme. What effect does this have?

DON PEDRO	Good morrow, masters. Put your torches out.
	The wolves have preyed, and look, the gentle day, **25**
	Before the wheels of Phoebus, round about
	Dapples the drowsy east with spots of grey.
	Thanks to you all, and leave us. Fare you well.
CLAUDIO	Good morrow, masters: each his several way.
DON PEDRO	Come, let us hence, and put on other weeds; **30**
	And then to Leonato's we will go.
CLAUDIO	And Hymen now with luckier issue speed's
	Than this for whom we rendered up this woe.

Exeunt.

In this scene ...

- Everyone gathers for the second wedding.
- Benedick states his desire to marry Beatrice.
- Hero is revealed to be alive. She and Claudio are reunited.
- Beatrice and Benedick publicly declare their affection for one another.
- A messenger arrives with news that Don John has been captured.

There is general joy that Hero's name has been cleared. Leonato sends the women to put on masks. Benedick asks Leonato for permission to marry Beatrice.

3 **debated**: explained

5 **against her will**: unintentionally
6 **question**: investigation

7 **sort**: turn out

8 **by faith**: i.e. he gave his word to Beatrice

14 **office**: job

THINK ABOUT for GCSE

Themes and issues

- **Wrongdoing, remorse and punishment**: How do you react to Leonato's comment that Don Pedro and Claudio are 'innocent' whereas 'Margaret was in some fault for this' (lines 2 to 6)? Is that your view too?

- **Men and women**: How far do you agree that Margaret is the only person among these three who should carry some blame?

17 **confirmed countenance**: straight face

18 **pains**: help

20 **undo**: ruin

24 **requite her**: return her feelings

At Leonato's house.

Enter LEONATO, ANTONIO, BENEDICK, BEATRICE, MARGARET, URSULA,
FRIAR FRANCIS *and* HERO.

FRIAR	Did I not tell you she was innocent?
LEONATO	So are the Prince and Claudio, who accused her Upon the error that you heard debated. But Margaret was in some fault for this, Although against her will, as it appears 5 In the true course of all the question.
ANTONIO	Well, I am glad that all things sort so well.
BENEDICK	And so am I, being else by faith enforced To call young Claudio to a reckoning for it.
LEONATO	Well, daughter, and you gentlewomen all, 10 Withdraw into a chamber by yourselves; And when I send for you, come hither masked. The Prince and Claudio promised by this hour To visit me. You know your office, brother: You must be father to your brother's daughter, 15 And give her to young Claudio.

Exit HERO, *with* BEATRICE, MARGARET *and* URSULA.

ANTONIO	Which I will do with confirmed countenance.
BENEDICK	Friar, I must entreat your pains, I think.
FRIAR	To do what, signior?
BENEDICK	To bind me, or undo me – one of them. 20 Signior Leonato: truth it is, good signior, Your niece regards me with an eye of favour.
LEONATO	That eye my daughter lent her. 'Tis most true.
BENEDICK	And I do with an eye of love requite her.
LEONATO	The sight whereof I think you had from me, 25 From Claudio, and the Prince. But what's your will?

Claudio arrives, believing that he is about to marry Antonio's daughter. Claudio and Don Pedro tease Benedick about his change of heart.

THINK ABOUT
for GCSE

Performance and staging

- Claudio's reply in line 38 is racist. In a recent production, Margaret was played by a black actress who remained on stage and reacted angrily. How would you deal with the line in a production?

Relationships

- According to Don Pedro, Benedick has 'a February face' (line 41), meaning that he looks cold and unwelcoming. Is Benedick friends with Claudio again, or is he still angry with him? What does their exchange in lines 43 to 52 suggest? Look at the use of 'thou' and 'you'.

Themes and issues

- **Love, courtship and marriage**: Compare lines 43 to 47 with Act 1 Scene 1, lines 221 to 222. What, according to Claudio, has love done to Benedick?

---

27 **enigmatical**: puzzling / mysterious

36 **yet**: still

38 **Ethiope**: In Shakespeare's time this was a term for any black African.

44 **tip ... gold**: make you a fine cuckold
45 **Europa**: Europe
46 **Europa**: A princess, carried off by Jupiter in the form of a bull.

48 **amiable low**: pleasing voice

50 **got**: fathered

52 **owe you**: will be even with you
   other reckonings: other accounts I must settle first

BENEDICK	Your answer, sir, is enigmatical.
	But, for my will, my will is your good will
	May stand with ours, this day to be conjoined
	In the state of honourable marriage –	30
	In which, good Friar, I shall desire your help.

| LEONATO | My heart is with your liking. |

| FRIAR | And my help. |
| | Here comes the Prince and Claudio. |

Enter DON PEDRO *and* CLAUDIO, *with attendants.*

| DON PEDRO | Good morrow to this fair assembly. |

LEONATO	Good morrow, Prince; good morrow, Claudio.	35
	We here attend you. Are you yet determined
	Today to marry with my brother's daughter?

| CLAUDIO | I'll hold my mind, were she an Ethiope. |

| LEONATO | Call her forth, brother; here's the Friar ready. |

Exit ANTONIO.

DON PEDRO	Good morrow, Benedick. Why, what's the matter,	40
	That you have such a February face,
	So full of frost, of storm and cloudiness?

CLAUDIO	I think he thinks upon the savage bull.
	Tush, fear not, man, we'll tip thy horns with gold,
	And all Europa shall rejoice at thee,	45
	As once Europa did at lusty Jove,
	When he would play the noble beast in love.

BENEDICK	Bull Jove, sir, had an amiable low –
	And some such strange bull leaped your father's cow,
	And got a calf in that same noble feat	50
	Much like to you, for you have just his bleat.

| CLAUDIO | For this I owe you. Here comes other reckonings. |

Enter ANTONIO, *with* HERO, BEATRICE, MARGARET *and* URSULA, *wearing masks.*

| | Which is the lady I must seize upon? |

| ANTONIO | This same is she, and I do give you her. |

At the wedding Claudio is amazed to discover that his bride is actually Hero. Beatrice and Benedick deny that they ever loved each other.

63 **defiled**: i.e. disgraced
64 **maid**: virgin

67 **qualify**: 1 moderate; 2 explain away

69 **largely**: in full detail
70 **let ... familiar**: treat this amazing event as an ordinary occurrence
71 **presently**: immediately
72 **Soft and fair**: i.e. Just a minute

THINK ABOUT for GCSE

Characterisation

* This is Hero's first appearance since her supposed death. Does she seem to be changed in any way?
* How do you imagine Hero is feeling at this time?

Performance and staging

* How would you direct an actress to play her speeches with Claudio?

81 **well-nigh**: almost

CLAUDIO	Why, then she's mine. Sweet, let me see your face. **55**
ANTONIO	No, that you shall not, till you take her hand Before this Friar, and swear to marry her.
CLAUDIO	Give me your hand: before this holy Friar, I am your husband, if you like of me.
HERO	(*Unmasking*) And when I lived, I was your other wife; **60** And when you loved, you were my other husband.
CLAUDIO	Another Hero!
HERO	Nothing certainer. One Hero died defiled, but I do live; And surely as I live I am a maid.
DON PEDRO	The former Hero! Hero that is dead! **65**
LEONATO	She died, my lord, but whiles her slander lived.
FRIAR	All this amazement can I qualify, When, after that the holy rites are ended, I'll tell you largely of fair Hero's death. Meantime let wonder seem familiar, **70** And to the chapel let us presently.
BENEDICK	Soft and fair, Friar. Which is Beatrice?
BEATRICE	(*Unmasking*) I answer to that name. What is your will?
BENEDICK	Do not you love me?
BEATRICE	Why no – no more than reason.
BENEDICK	Why, then your uncle and the Prince and Claudio **75** Have been deceived. They swore you did.
BEATRICE	Do not you love me?
BENEDICK	Troth, no – no more than reason.
BEATRICE	Why, then my cousin, Margaret and Ursula Are much deceived: for they did swear you did.
BENEDICK	They swore that you were almost sick for me. **80**
BEATRICE	They swore that you were well-nigh dead for me.
BENEDICK	'Tis no such matter. Then you do not love me?

Claudio and Hero produce love poems written by Beatrice and Benedick proving their love for one another.

83   **but ... recompense**: only as friends

87   **halting**: lamely written

96   **in a consumption**: i.e. dying for love of me

100   **flout**: mock
101   **care for**: am hurt by
       satire ... epigram: i.e. empty mocking words
103   **purpose**: intend

106   **giddy**: changeable

111   **cudgelled**: beaten
112   **double-dealer**: 1 someone who has a partner; 2 deceiver
113–14 **look ... to**: keep a close eye on

THINK ABOUT for GCSE

Characterisation

• What is Claudio implying about Benedick in lines 110 to 114?

Performance and staging

• How do you think Benedick should say 'Come, come, we are friends' (line 115)?

BEATRICE	No, truly, but in friendly recompense.
LEONATO	Come, cousin, I am sure you love the gentleman.
CLAUDIO	And I'll be sworn upon't that he loves her; 85 For here's a paper written in his hand, A halting sonnet of his own pure brain, Fashioned to Beatrice.
HERO	And here's another, Writ in my cousin's hand, stolen from her pocket, Containing her affection unto Benedick. 90
BENEDICK	A miracle! Here's our own hands against our hearts. Come, I will have thee: but, by this light, I take thee for pity.
BEATRICE	I would not deny you; but, by this good day, I yield upon great persuasion – and partly to save your life, 95 for I was told you were in a consumption.
BENEDICK	Peace! I will stop your mouth. (***Kissing her***)
DON PEDRO	How dost thou, Benedick the married man?
BENEDICK	I'll tell thee what, Prince. A college of wit-crackers cannot flout me out of my humour. Dost thou think I 100 care for a satire or an epigram? No: if a man will be beaten with brains, 'a shall wear nothing handsome about him. In brief, since I do purpose to marry, I will think nothing to any purpose that the world can say against it. And therefore never flout at me for what I 105 have said against it – for man is a giddy thing, and this is my conclusion. For thy part, Claudio, I did think to have beaten thee: but in that thou art like to be my kinsman, live unbruised, and love my cousin.
CLAUDIO	I had well hoped, thou wouldst have denied Beatrice, 110 that I might have cudgelled thee out of thy single life, to make thee a double-dealer – which out of question thou wilt be, if my cousin do not look exceeding narrowly to thee.
BENEDICK	Come, come, we are friends. Let's have a dance ere 115 we are married, that we may lighten our own hearts and our wives' heels.

Benedick proposes a dance before the wedding ceremony. A messenger brings word that Don John has been arrested. He will be punished after the weddings have taken place.

120–1 There ... horn: A last cuckold joke.

THINK ABOUT for GCSE

Performance and staging

124 brave: great

- In one production, Beatrice and Benedick carried on arguing during the dance which ends the play and didn't notice that the other characters had left. How would you end the play?
- How 'sad' should Don Pedro appear? What should he do at the end of the play?

Relationships

- What differences can you see between the two relationships – Hero and Claudio, and Beatrice and Benedick? Think about the characters themselves, the different routes by which each pair came together, and the obstacles they have had to overcome.

Themes and issues

- **Wrongdoing, remorse and punishment**: What exactly has Don John done wrong? What 'brave punishments' does he deserve, in your opinion? Does anyone else deserve to be punished?

LEONATO   We'll have dancing afterward.

BENEDICK   First, of my word! Therefore play, music. Prince, thou
               art sad: get thee a wife, get thee a wife! There is no   120
               staff more reverend than one tipped with horn.

               Enter a MESSENGER.

MESSENGER   My lord, your brother John is ta'en in flight,
               And brought with armed men back to Messina.

BENEDICK   Think not on him till tomorrow. I'll devise thee brave
               punishments for him. Strike up, pipers!   125

                                                              Dance.

                                                              Exeunt.

Much Ado About Nothing is a comedy about love and deception. It takes place in Messina, Italy, and revolves around a funny and high-spirited group of people – in particular, Beatrice and Benedick. These two characters are the stars of the play, even though many of the dramatic events centre around the young lovers Hero and Claudio. During Shakespeare's lifetime the play was sometimes referred to as 'Beatrice and Benedick'.

COMEDY

Shakespeare's comedies focus on the lighter aspects of life and often include dances and songs. Villains and mischievous schemes feature in them, but there are no real tragedies or deaths, and the plot moves towards a happy ending. Unlike the tragedies they begin with chaos and end in order. They centre on love and courtship and usually end with a wedding about to take place. In all the comedies, the women are wiser than the men about the nature of love and relationships. The men have to grow up and learn the meaning of true love. The comedies also contain humorous, often lower-class, characters such as Dogberry, the bungling town constable, who misuses important-sounding words with comic effect.

LOVE AND COURTSHIP

In Shakespeare's time it was common for marriage to be as much about money and social connections as love. Marriages were often, for example, arranged by the fathers, rather than the couples themselves, especially among the wealthier classes. In *Much Ado About Nothing*, the two couples show two different attitudes towards courtship, the ritual that leads towards marriage. The courtship of one couple is very traditional, whilst the other seems less conventional and perhaps more modern.

When the young Claudio falls in love with Hero, he also asks Don Pedro (his commanding officer) whether Leonato has any other children. He wants to know whether Hero will inherit all her father's wealth. Since Don Pedro is a powerful and important figure, he offers to speak to Leonato and Hero on Claudio's behalf. In fact, Claudio and Hero hardly ever speak to each other in the play and are never alone together. With Beatrice and Benedick, however, it is different. They have known each other for some time, and once they have realised that they are in love, they speak to each other openly about it. Their relationship is founded on love and trust, even though they continue to argue. Even Benedick, though, follows the rules. He asks Leonato, Beatrice's guardian, for his permission to marry her.

HONOUR

Messina is a male-dominated society, like Shakespearean England. The idea of honour, or reputation, was different for men and women. For men it was based on family, class and reputation among other men. For women it depended on being sexually pure. Men could defend their honour by challenging another man to a duel, but this option was not open to women – they had to depend upon men to uphold their honour for them. Hero's honour is challenged by Claudio when he accuses her of being unfaithful. Leonato, her father, does not immediately try to defend her because he is more concerned about his status as father and dignity among the other men. Honour would come to Leonato if his daughter married a friend of the Prince, Don Pedro, the character with the highest status in the play.

THE VILLAIN

The comedies usually contain a character or situation that threatens the happiness of the lovers. In *Much Ado About Nothing*, this takes the shape of the spiteful Don John. Don John is a *malcontent*: he makes trouble even when there is nothing to gain by it. He is an illegitimate son (the stage directions call him the 'Bastard'). Shakespeare's audiences would have understood the anger of illegitimate sons who would not inherit their fathers' lands or titles. Because this is a comedy, however, Don John does not finally triumph. He is arrested before he can do any real harm and he is missing from the happy ending.

THEATRE AND STAGE

Much Ado About Nothing probably dates from 1598. Its earliest performances may well have been in the theatre called the Curtain, in Shoreditch, on what was then the north-east edge of London. This was where Shakespeare's acting company (known then as the Lord Chamberlain's Men) performed temporarily before moving to their new home at the Globe playhouse in 1599. Built back in 1577, the Curtain was 'old', shabbier and perhaps rather smaller than the famous Globe, but it was a playhouse of the same familiar Elizabethan type. It would have had the same large stage (maybe about twelve metres wide by eight metres deep), surrounded by an open yard and covered galleries for spectators. A reconstruction of the Curtain (showing a performance of *Romeo and Juliet*) was featured in the film *Shakespeare in Love* (1998).

What we know about the early staging of *Much Ado About Nothing* comes from the evidence of the play itself. All the action takes place on the large main stage – and this was clearly big enough for characters to appear on it in separate groups, to 'hide' themselves from others, and to overhear (or *not* to overhear) what others say, depending on their stage positions. In the opening scene, Don Pedro and Leonato 'move aside' to talk together, while the wit-battle of Benedick and Beatrice takes centre-stage. In Act 3 Scene 3, Borachio tells Conrade of the 'villainy' he and Don John have carried out against Hero, unaware that he is being overheard by Constable Dogberry's men. When Benedick challenges Claudio to fight, in Act 5 Scene 1, Don Pedro is clearly not close enough to realise at first ('What, a feast, a feast?') the seriousness of what is happening between them.

SCENES, SETTINGS AND PROPS

The action of the play in an Elizabethan theatre would have been fast and continuous, with no intervals between acts or scenes. New scenes are often marked simply by the entrance of new characters. Act 3 Scene 3, for instance, ends with the arrest of Conrade and Borachio by the Watchmen. Then as Hero, Margaret and Ursula enter discussing Hero's wedding preparations, a new scene begins in a new imaginary setting: indoors, inside Leonato's house. No scenery or stage lighting, as we think of them, was used. The play's language and activity were enough to suggest places and settings to the imagination of its audience.

Leonato's house, around which the action of *Much Ado About Nothing* revolves, would have been represented from 'outside' only by the rising wall of the dressing-room area behind the stage, where the two main stage entrances would have suggested its doors. The same stage-architecture would have been enough to suggest a 'church' interior when Friar Francis stands before it to begin the wedding ceremony for Hero and Claudio in Act 4 Scene 1.

Other settings are often indicated only by which characters appear and by what they say or do, although some basic props might also have been brought out onto the stage. A difference is signalled for the comic scene in which Dogberry and the Sexton 'examine' their prisoners Conrade and Borachio (Act 4 Scene 2). Here, 'gowns' for the important 'examiners', stools (with 'a cushion for the Sexton'), and probably a table would have been enough to suggest action in the local prison (although no actual location is mentioned). When Claudio mourns for Hero, in Act 5 Scene 3, the audience would again have imagined action inside 'the church'. Candles or burning torches were not used in this scene for lighting, but to tell the audience, in the open-air afternoon daylight of an Elizabethan theatre, that it was watching a night-time scene. Leonato's family 'monument' (the tomb supposedly containing Hero's body) may have been a central recess in the back wall of the stage or, possibly, a 'tomb' prop may have been briefly pushed out for this scene.

'Overhearing' scenes are vital to the comedy and plot of *Much Ado About Nothing*. In the two famous 'garden' scenes (Act 2 Scene 3 and Act 3 Scene 1), Benedick and Beatrice hide, in turn, to overhear what is said about them by other characters who know well enough that they are there. The language and activity of these scenes is enough to suggest that the main-stage setting is now to be imagined as 'Leonato's garden' or 'orchard'. It would have been possible, at the simplest, to have played the scenes with Benedick or Beatrice lurking behind one of the pillars holding up the canopy over the stage. But Elizabethan theatres did sometimes use artificial frames of leaves, as well as 'banks of moss' or small 'trees' to represent bowers or arbours. The vital 'overhearing' which leads to the arrest of Conrade and Borachio and the eventual exposure of Don John's 'villainy' (Act 3 Scene 3) is more clearly located. As they meet, in imaginary darkness,

Borachio tells Conrade to stand 'under this pent-house, for it drizzles rain'. This suggests a position just under the sheltering overhang of the stage canopy, while the Watchmen listen from behind or from the other side of the stage. Overhearings under the overhang of houses gave the original meaning to our word 'eavesdropping' – and sometimes, of course, it really would have 'drizzled rain' into the open yard of an Elizabethan theatre.

Fashion, music and language

It is no accident, in *Much Ado About Nothing,* that a scene in which Borachio mocks at 'giddy' changes in fashion is followed at once by one in which the 'rare fashion' of Hero's gown for her wedding is discussed (Act 3 Scene 4). The wedding will also be subject to a sudden disturbing 'change'.

Costumes were important signals of character, social class and setting for audiences in an Elizabethan theatre. They were also the most valuable part of any theatre company's equipment, often costing far more than the sums paid to writers for providing plays. Clothes were a measure of rank and wealth. Only 'gentlemen', for example, were entitled to wear swords, and servants would wear the livery (badge or uniform colour) of their masters. A comedy of love involving a Prince and a Count would demand the display of rich and colourful costumes. It may well have delighted class-conscious Elizabethan audiences, too, that Dogberry's humbly-dressed working-class Watchmen (however bumbling and funny themselves) could manage the important arrest of villainous 'gentlemen'.

Apart from Don John's plotting and the seriousness of the 'shaming' of Hero, *Much Ado About Nothing* is a generally light-hearted comedy of love. Like other love-comedies by Shakespeare, it clearly shows the pleasure that early audiences took in varieties of language and music. Eyewitness accounts by visitors to Elizabethan theatres praise the quality of music and 'elegant' dancing they heard and saw there. The musicians of the company might play in the gallery above and behind the stage, or sometimes on the stage itself. *Much Ado About Nothing* also has one of Shakespeare's most beautiful and significant songs ('Sigh no more, ladies', in Act 2 Scene 3). Many Elizabethan actors were also skilful musicians themselves, and Balthasar's performance would probably have been a show-piece of singing to accompaniment on a lute.

The language of the play shows a typical intense enjoyment in joking and playing with words. Combats of wit between Beatrice and Benedick are a main attraction – and the part of Beatrice, in particular, demonstrates the skill of the specialist boy actors who played the young women of Shakespeare's plays. The variety of this comedy also extends to the almost tragic passion of Leonato's response to the crisis that engulfs his daughter's wedding and the part of pompous Dogberry, with his misuse of words, which was created for Will Kemp, the starring clown of Shakespeare's acting company in the 1590s.

Staging in Shakespeare's theatre may in some ways seem crude or simple by modern standards, but it was extremely powerful in playing to the imaginations and enjoyment of its audiences. *Much Ado About Nothing*, led by the 'giddy' starring roles of Benedick and Beatrice, had all the theatrical ingredients to make it a lasting popular success.

A play in performance at the reconstruction of Shakespeare's Globe

Much Ado About Nothing is one of five plays Shakespeare wrote about a jealous man wrongly suspecting an innocent woman of being unfaithful. Although disaster is avoided, the scene in which Claudio publicly condemns Hero brings the story close to tragedy. Shortly afterwards, Beatrice draws the battle lines of the war between the sexes when she asks Benedick to 'Kill Claudio'. However, Shakespeare balances the seriousness of this scene with the comic actions of Dogberry and his crew, and all ends well with a dance and the promise of a double wedding.

A number of Shakespeare's military figures, who only know how to be soldiers, seem uncomfortably out of place in peacetime. Don John, the villain of the play, bears grudges from the battlefield, but in many productions we are given the impression that Claudio believes his lies about Hero because he is a fellow soldier. At first, Benedick is disappointed that Claudio changes from a soldier to a lover, but when he himself falls in love, he puts his relationship with Beatrice above his loyalty to his army friends, supporting Hero's cause.

Directors and designers have chosen a wide variety of settings for this comedy, including the Italian Renaissance, the American Civil War, the 1920s, the 1940s and modern Sicily, but the productions have in common key elements of the play:

- the exciting and disruptive presence of soldiers in Messina, a civilian setting
- men and the military, and the importance of honour
- love and courtship.

MESSINA

Several productions have chosen the Jane Austen era as a setting; the play's themes are similar to those in Austen's novels. Like the handsome officers of *Pride and Prejudice* and *Persuasion*, Don Pedro's men are glamorous visitors in uniform, for whom the horrors of war are remote. Audiences can find a parallel between Beatrice and Benedick, and Elizabeth Bennett and Mr Darcy, both in their witty banter and in the changes of mind and heart that all four characters undergo.

In **Kenneth Branagh**'s film (1993), shot in the picturesque Italian countryside and set in the early 19th century, Messina is a happy, relaxed environment where people laugh and enjoy life in the sunshine. The arrival of Don Pedro's band of soldiers, in their crisp white and navy uniforms, is treated as an opportunity for romance to blossom between the soldiers and the local ladies. The soldiers are welcomed as old friends, and Hero's outdoor wedding is a celebration to which the whole community is invited. Social distinctions seem unimportant – until Claudio and Don Pedro accuse Hero and turn against Leonato. Despite the fact that he is the governor of Messina, Leonato is powerless against the Prince to right his daughter's wrongs.

In the BBC production (1984, directed by **Stuart Burge**), set in an Italian Renaissance palace with rich costumes of gold-embroidered silks, Messina is an important seat of government where people flirt by means of carefully choreographed, formal dances. The soldiers arrive, grimy from battle, but quickly change out of their military wear into what seem to be the fashions of Messina. Hero's wedding takes place (or rather, does not take place) in an ornate church full of stained glass windows and carved columns, and everyone is dressed in their best. Claudio's denunciation of Hero is not only socially destructive, but it also seems a violation of a sacred place.

In a Shakespeare Theater, Washington, D.C. production (2003), the director **Mark Lamos** set the story in the 'roaring '20s' Beatrice was a flapper, the soldiers were flying aces, and Leonato was an old-fashioned uncle and father who strongly disapproved of Beatrice's dislike of men and marriage. Gershwin-style dance tunes helped set the mood for a world of champagne, parties and witty conversation. Hero, who initially appeared to be quite a conventional and demure young lady, gained more strength of character in the course of the play – by the end, she seemed more 'modern', like Beatrice.

A Regent's Park production (2000, directed by **Rachel Kavanaugh**) re-imagined Messina as an English country house during World War II. The women and older men stayed home while the younger men fought – although the second World War is a much more serious setting than Shakespeare's quick description of a battle that lost 'few of any sort, and none of name'. Dogberry's crew was closely based on the characters in *Dad's Army*; Margaret and Ursula were land girls (young women volunteer farm-workers); and Don Pedro's soldiers were handsome heroes of the Battle of Britain. Again, music helped to create the setting as big band tunes fuelled the wartime romances.

MEN AND THE MILITARY

In many productions, Claudio looks much younger than Benedick and Don Pedro. Although he has distinguished himself in the recent war, he has relatively little experience in battle, and has even less experience with love. In the 2000 **Regent's Park** production, Claudio looked up to Don Pedro as his commanding officer in all important matters. When Don Pedro joked about Benedick falling in love, Claudio followed his lead. In this production, the soldiers' uniforms helped to clarify the characters. Benedick wore civilian clothes in the less formal scenes, but Don Pedro, ever the officer, stayed in the military clothing that demonstrated his rank. Benedick put on his uniform again when he challenged Claudio to a duel, to show the seriousness of the situation, and in the same scene he resigned from Don Pedro's regiment.

In the **Branagh** film, Benedick, Claudio, and Don Pedro are close friends, and Benedick seems to feel a sense of betrayal when Claudio announces his love for Hero. Branagh plays Benedick for every laugh in the early scenes, but becomes deadly serious when challenging Claudio to the duel.

LOVE AND COURTSHIP

Although Hero and Claudio are sometimes considered to be the main plot of the play, Beatrice and Benedick are the real stars of the show. It is difficult from the text to determine whom Hero likes at the beginning of the play, and Claudio himself admits that he is not a very demonstrative wooer. Beatrice and Benedick, on the other hand, seem obsessed with each other, despite what they say publicly. While Hero seems ready to accept Don Pedro when he asks for her hand to give to Claudio, Beatrice shows her independence by refusing Don Pedro, the best offer of marriage she is ever likely to receive. In some productions, Don Pedro's offer is a serious one, in others it is no more than light-hearted banter. While this moment is treated lightly in the **BBC** production, with Don Pedro hiding his face behind an ugly mask, it is real in the **Branagh** film, with Beatrice gently trying to spare Don Pedro's feelings.

Actors playing Beatrice and Benedick often prepare for these roles by discussing a possible history between the characters. Shakespeare gives actors some clues about an unsuccessful romantic relationship in the opening scenes. Kenneth Branagh and Emma Thompson, real-life husband and wife when Branagh filmed *Much Ado About Nothing*, capture both the sharp wit and the loving camaraderie in their portrayal of Beatrice and Benedick. In their first scene together, she establishes the sense of a history between them with her wistful 'I know you of old', a line that Cherie Lunghi speaks more bitterly in the **BBC** production. Her Beatrice snaps out, 'Do not swear and eat it', when Benedick declares his love, suggesting that he has broken his word to her in the past and now has to prove his trustworthiness. Robert Lindsay's Benedick responds to her 'Kill Claudio' with an attempt at a laugh, and an indignant 'Not for the wide world', but his ultimate promise to challenge Claudio shows sincere love and devotion to Beatrice. In an all-female production of the play at **Shakespeare's Globe, London** (2004), Josie Lawrence's Benedick showed the seriousness of Beatrice's demand that he kill Claudio in an unusual fashion. When Benedick joked about a man building his own tomb (Act 5 Scene 2), a light-hearted bit of banter in most productions, Yolanda Vasquez's Beatrice suddenly realised that he might die in the duel that she demanded of him.

A few productions have cast somewhat older actors as the battling couple, in an interpretation that suggests that neither has married because they are too proud or shy to admit their feelings for the other. Judi Dench and Harriet Walter were two Beatrices fitting this description; being significantly older than Hero, Beatrice became more of a mother figure to her cousin. Their Benedicks, Donald Sinden and Nicholas Le Prevost, were confirmed old bachelors to whom the military life seemed their only option. The sense of a rocky history between the two, and the resulting concern about exposing their feelings, can be more powerful when the characters are older and this may be their last chance for love.

Assessment of Shakespeare in your English Literature GCSE

All students studying GCSE English Literature have to study at least six texts, three of which are from the English, Welsh or Irish literary heritage. These texts must include prose, poetry and drama, and in England this must include a play by Shakespeare.

The four major exam boards: AQA, Edexcel, WJEC and OCR, include Shakespeare as part of their specifications for English Literature. All the exam boards offer controlled assessment to assess their students' understanding of Shakespeare, although some offer a traditional examination as an alternative option, or as one element of the assessment.

This section of the book offers guidance and support to help you prepare for your GCSE assessment on Shakespeare. The first part (pages 196–8) is relevant to all students, whichever exam board's course you are taking. The second part (pages 199–216) is board-specific, and you should turn to those pages that are relevant to your exam board. Your teacher will advise you if you are unsure which board you are working with.

What you will be assessed on

In your English Literature GCSE you will be marked on various Assessment Objectives (AOs). These assess your ability to:

- **AO1: respond to texts critically and imaginatively; select and evaluate relevant textual detail to illustrate and support interpretations**
  This means that you should show insight and imagination when writing about the text, showing understanding of what the author is saying and how he or she is saying it; and use quotations or direct references to the text to support your ideas and point of view.

- **AO2: explain how language, structure and form contribute to writers' presentation of ideas, themes and settings**
  This means that you need to explain how writers use language (vocabulary, imagery and other literary features), structure and form (the 'shape' of the text) to present ideas, themes and settings (where the action takes place).

- **AO3: make comparisons and explain links between texts, evaluating writers' different ways of expressing meaning and achieving effects**
  This means that you compare and link texts, identifying what they have in common and looking at how different writers express meaning and create specific effects for the reader/audience.

- **AO4: relate texts to their social, cultural and historical contexts; explain how texts have been influential and significant to self and other readers in different contexts and at different times**
  This means that, where it is relevant, you need to show awareness of the social, cultural and historical background of the texts; explain the influence of texts on yourself and other readers in different places and times.

You will also be assessed on the **Quality of your Written Communication**. This means you need to ensure that: your text is legible and your spelling, punctuation and grammar are accurate so that the meaning is clear; you choose a style of writing that is suitable for the task; you organise information clearly and logically, using specialist words where relevant.

Not all exam boards assess all the AOs as part of the English Literature Shakespeare task. Here is a summary:

Exam Board	Unit	AO1	AO2	AO3	AO4
AQA	Unit 3 CA	✓	✓	✓	✓
	Unit 4 Exam	✓	✓		
Edexcel	Unit 3 CA		✓	✓	
WJEC	Unit 2 Exam	✓	✓		✓

WHAT IS CONTROLLED ASSESSMENT?

Controlled assessment is a way of testing students' knowledge and ability. It differs from an examination in that you will be given the task in advance so you can research and prepare for it, before sitting down to write a full response to it under supervised conditions.

Exam boards differ in the detail of their controlled assessment rules, so do check them out in the board-specific section. However, the general stages of controlled assessment are as follows:

1. The task
   Every year exam boards either set a specific task or offer a choice. Your teacher might adapt one of the tasks to suit you and the resources available. You will be given this task well in advance of having to respond to it, so you have plenty of time to prepare for it.

2. Planning and research

Your teacher will have helped you study your text and taught you how to approach the topics. He or she will now advise you on how to carry out further research and plan for your task.

- During this phase you can work with others, for example discussing ideas and sharing resources on the internet.

- Your teacher can give you general feedback during this phase, but not detailed advice.

- You must keep a record of all the source materials you use, including websites.

3. Writing up the response

This will take place under timed, supervised conditions.

- It may be split into more than one session, in which case your teacher will collect your work at the end of the session and put it away until the beginning of the next. You will not have access to it between sessions.

- You may be allowed to take an **un-annotated copy** of the text into the session.

- You may be allowed to take in some brief **notes**.

- You may be allowed access to a **dictionary** or a **thesaurus**.

- You may be allowed to produce your assessment on a computer, but you will not be allowed access to the internet, email, disks or memory sticks.

- During this time, you may not communicate with other candidates. The work you produce must be entirely **your own**.

- Your teacher will advise you on how much you should aim to write.

4. Marking

Your Controlled Assessment Task will be marked by your teacher and may be moderated (supervised and checked) by your exam board.

General examiners' note

Remember:

- you will get marks for responding to the task, but not for writing other material that is not relevant

- you must produce an **individual** response to the task in the final assessment, even if you have discussed ideas with other students previously.

How to succeed in AQA English Literature

Your teachers will decide whether you should write about *Much Ado About Nothing* in a Controlled Assessment Task (Unit 3) or an Examination (Unit 4). These two units are very different, so you need to be absolutely sure which one you are taking. If you are in any doubt, ask your teacher.

> ### Examiner's tip
> You will be assessed on the following objectives when responding to your Shakespeare task in the Unit 3 Controlled Assessment: AO1, AO2, AO3, AO4. Refer back to pages 196–7 for more about these assessment objectives.
>
> (AO3 and AO4 are not relevant if you are taking the Unit 4 Exam.)

Unit 3 Controlled Assessment Task

If you take this unit, you have to write about a Shakespeare play and one other text that your teacher will choose. It may be a novel, a selection of poetry, another play or even another Shakespeare play. The two texts will be linked in some way and you are expected to write about both.

The task

AQA will give your teacher a number of tasks to choose from. There are two main topics:

1. **Themes and ideas**

   These tasks might involve writing about love or hate, conflict or power, families or outsiders. For example: *Explore the ways writers present different aspects of love in the texts you have studied* **or** *Explore the ways writers present and use ideas of loyalty and betrayal in the texts you have studied.*

2. **Characterisation and voice**

   These tasks might involve writing about relationships, parents and children, comic characters, or old people. For example: *Explore the ways writers present lovers in the texts you have studied* **or** *Explore the ways writers show how people can be tricked by others in the texts you have studied.*

Your response

- You have to complete a written response to ONE task. This should be about 2,000 words but remember that it's quality not quantity that counts.
- You have FOUR hours to produce your work. Your teacher will probably ask you to complete the task over separate sessions rather than in a single sitting.

- Your teacher will give you plenty of time to prepare for the task. You can use any resources you like, but do keep a record of them (including websites). You must include a list of these at the end of your task.
- You can work in a small group to research and prepare your material but your final work must be all your own.
- Do watch different versions of the play. You can refer to the different versions when you write your response and you will be given credit for this.
- You can refer to brief notes when you are writing your response, but these must be brief. You must hand in your notes in at the end of each session and on completion of the task. You can also use a copy of the play without any annotations.
- You can handwrite your response or use a word processor. You are allowed a dictionary and thesaurus or grammar and spell-check programs. You are NOT allowed to use the internet, email, disks or memory sticks when writing your response.
- You can do the Controlled Assessment Task in January or June. When you have finished, your teachers will mark your work and then send a sample from your school to AQA to be checked.

Examiner's tip
The Controlled Assessment Task is worth 25 per cent of your final English Literature mark – so it's worth doing it well.

HOW TO GET A GOOD GRADE

1. Select what you write about carefully. It is better to write a lot about a little. Concentrate on one scene in Shakespeare and one chapter in a novel or a single poem, or on two characters, one from a Shakespeare play and one from a novel.
2. Use short, relevant quotations. Every time you include a quotation, consider the language the writer has used and the probable effect on the audience.
3. Never retell the story. You and your teachers already know it. If you find yourself doing this, stop and refocus on the question.
4. Check your spellings, in particular writers' and characters' names.
5. Always remember that Beatrice, Benedick and the other characters in the play are not real. Do not write about them as if they are. They have been created by Shakespeare: his play is the important thing to consider.

SAMPLE CONTROLLED ASSESSMENT TASK

> Explore the ways writers present different aspects of love.

Here are extracts from responses written by two students. Both are writing about the dialogue between Benedick, Claudio and Don Pedro in Act 1 Scene 1.

Extract 1 – Grade C response

Relevant textual detail

In this dialogue the three characters are talking about love. Claudio has fallen in love with Hero. He tells the others 'That I love her, I feel'. Benedick makes fun of him but then the other two turn on Benedick and accuse him of being unable to love. Claudio says that he is just acting as though he hates all women. Benedick says that he is pleased that he was born and brought up by a woman but that he wants to live as a bachelor. When Don Pedro says that one day Benedick will fall in love, Benedick says that if he ever does, 'hang me in a bottle like a cat' which refers to the bottles used as target practice by archers. This also refers to the idea that Cupid fires arrows, though he is blind so they could land anywhere. This is why people fall in love for little reason.

Explains effect

Sustains explanation

Explains effect

Good point but needs further development

Examiner's comments

- The student clearly understands some of Shakespeare's ideas and uses of language in the speech.
- Not all points are fully explained and backed up; for example, Benedick's assertion that he will live as a bachelor, or the image of Cupid's arrows.
- There is a general understanding of how Benedick sees love, although the effects of this on the other characters and the audience are not really considered.
- This is a Grade C response. To improve, this student needs to develop ideas in more detail and to link these details to a more thoughtful consideration of the scene.

Extract 2 – Grade A response

Clear, detailed statement

The role which the seemingly cynical Benedick has chosen to adopt is highly theatrical: it is as if he is directing a scene in which he is to be the star. He even provides Don Pedro with the dialogue: 'Now that is your Grace's part'.

Awareness of effect on audience

This is both respectful, for he uses Don Pedro's title, and disrespectful, as he is telling Don Pedro what to say.

Exploration of language

It is perhaps slightly disappointing that the joke Benedick has so carefully built up is so disappointing: a pun on 'short' and a reference to Hero's size. That said, Claudio admits that 'If this were so, so were it uttered', a clever and delicately balanced line with its repeated 'er' and 't' sounds which implies that Benedick would always mock any such feelings.

Analytic use of detail

Don Pedro tells him, 'Thou wast ever an obstinate heretic in the despite of beauty', playing with the image Benedick has used of dying at the stake.

Insight into themes

Both characters are equating love of beauty with religion: to love beauty is to be orthodox and acceptable; to ignore it is to risk censure and even death. In a play in which love and death become fused, this might be ominous.

Insight into character

However, Claudio breaks any tension by reminding the audience that Benedick 'never could maintain his part but in the force of his will': Benedick is only playing a character. He is the star of his own show.

Examiner's comments

- The student shows a clear engagement with Shakespeare's ideas and the attitudes of Benedick.
- There is evidence of a sophisticated interpretation and a perceptive exploration of Shakespeare's use of language.
- This is a Grade A response. The student has written a lot about a little but has also explored some of the themes of the text as a whole.

UNIT 4 EXAMINATION

If you take Unit 4 in your AQA English Literature course then you will answer a question on a Shakespeare play in an examination. Your answer is worth 20 per cent of your total Literature mark and you will need to spend about 40 minutes on this question.

The Shakespeare question will always have **two** parts. Each is worth 10 per cent of your total mark so you must spend equal time on them.

- **Part (a)** of each question will ask you to write about a specific extract. This extract may be a monologue (spoken by one character) or a part of a scene where two or more characters are talking.
- **Part (b)** of each question will ask you to write about the same topic but as it relates to a different part of the play (there will not be a printed extract in the exam paper to refer to).

Part (a)	How does Shakespeare show Beatrice's thoughts and feelings in the extract below?
	Extract: Act 3 Scene 1, lines 107-116 (page 85)
From:	What fire is in mine ears? Can this be true? ...
To:	... Believe it better than reportingly.
Part (b)	How does Shakespeare show Beatrice's feelings in a different part of the play?

Examiner's tip

The first part of each question asks '*How does Shakespeare . . .?*' The 'how' is important. It means you must consider Shakespeare's use of language, referring to specific words and phrases and the effects these create.

Here are extracts from essays by two students. Both are answering Part (a) of the question on *Much Ado About Nothing*.

Extract 1 – Grade C response

Understanding of context

Apt response to character

Explanation of effects on audience

In this soliloquy Beatrice has just been listening to Hero and Ursula pretending that Benedick is in love with her. They are doing this because Beatrice and Benedick are always quarrelling and everyone else thought it would be funny to trick them into thinking that the other one loved them. Beatrice is very quick to believe what they say and says 'What fire is in mine ears?'. This means that she thinks her ears have gone red because people have been talking about her. She is also very surprised that everyone thinks she is such a proud person. She repeats the word 'pride' to emphasise that she is not going to be proud anymore and so she wishes it 'adieu' or 'goodbye'. She then says that she will be a tame bird and that Benedick will control her. If he really does love her, then she will make sure that they get married. The audience thinks that it will be funny to see them both in love when they have been fighting each other so much.

Appropriate comment on image

Sustained response to language

Examiner's comments

* The ideas here are expressed clearly, appropriately and in context.
* The response is sustained, providing examples of Shakespeare's use of language, but comments on these need to be developed.
* It briefly considers the effect the speech would have on the audience.
* This is a Grade C response. To improve, this student must develop ideas in more detail and link details to an interpretation of the whole speech.

Extract 2 – Grade A response

In this soliloquy the audience is presented with a completely new Beatrice. Gone is the young woman who knows her own mind and is never afraid to express it. This Beatrice is so fooled by Hero and Ursula that she immediately promises to 'tame' herself. Her acceptance of the new order is certainly sudden and this change is shown in a new pattern of speech. Gone is the prose the audience has come to expect and instead Beatrice uses an abbreviated sonnet. 'Condemned' is cleverly mirrored in 'contempt' which she declares she will banish, and the key line 'Taming my wild heart to thy loving hand' creates the image of her as a wild bird being prepared to be subservient to Benedick's command. No matter how loving he may be, there is perhaps something of a disappointment in seeing an independent young woman preparing herself to be tamed by a man even though she claims that she will ensure that they are married: 'To bind our loves up in a holy band', the image of the wedding ring echoing the image of the knot though there is a suggestion that the 'loves' may be different and need binding together. Shakespeare has already hinted that they have had an affair which did not work. Here there is a sense of Beatrice trying to revive the romantic language of her past, as in the dreadful rhyme of 'requite thee' and 'incite thee'. Perhaps she is a little too old to use sonnets.

Marginal notes: Clear interpretation; Analytic use of detail; Good analysis of language; Shows insight and interpretation

Examiner's comments

- In this response the ideas are expressed cogently and persuasively and text references are apt.
- There is evidence of imagination in the development of the interpretation and there is a confident exploration of Shakespeare's use of language.
- The student has written a lot about a little but has also managed to explore some of the themes of the text as a whole.
- This is a Grade A response.

How to succeed in Edexcel English Literature

The response to Shakespeare in Edexcel GCSE English Literature is a Controlled Assessment Task. You must produce your work at school or college under supervision and within two hours, although you may do some preparation for it in advance.

The task

The task will ask you to compare and make links between your own reading of the Shakespeare text and an adaptation. The adaptation can be a film, TV production, musical, graphic novel, audio version or a cartoon, but all must be based on the original play. The task will focus on **one** of the following aspects of the play:

- **Characterisation**
  For example, a study of the importance and development of **one** of the main characters in *Much Ado About Nothing*.

- **Stagecraft**
  For example, looking at ways in which the decisions taken about the staging and set influence the production.

- **Theme**
  For example, following how the action of the play is affected by a central theme such as love, deception or honour.

- **Relationships**
  For example, Hero and Claudio, Beatrice and Benedick or Beatrice and Hero.

Note that your answer should include some discussion of dramatic devices. These include a range of theatrical techniques and styles used by the playwright to create a particular effect on the audience, such as soliloquies, monologues; juxtaposition and contrast; use of dramatic irony; use of the stage and props; actions and reactions.

Preparing your response

When preparing, you will be able to use a range of resources available at your centre, which may include the internet, TV, videos and film, live performances and notes made in class.

You must complete your tasks individually, without intervention or assistance from others. However, you will be able to use: copies of the text without any annotations written in them; notes (bullet or numbered points), but not a prepared draft or continuous phrases/sentences or paragraphs); a dictionary or thesaurus; grammar or spell-check programs.

Examiner's tip
If possible, see several different adaptations of *Much Ado About Nothing* and compare the ways they treat the story and characters.

HOW TO GET A GOOD GRADE

To get a good mark in this response, it is important that you:

- respond to the chosen drama text critically and imaginatively
- make comparisons and explain links with your own reading
- look at different ways that a production or adaptation expresses ideas
- consider what Shakespeare means and how he achieves his effects
- support your ideas by including evidence from the words of the play.

ACTIVITIES

The following approaches will help you to explore *Much Ado About Nothing* in preparation for the controlled assessment.

Activity 1: Characterisation

Draw up a page with two columns, one for Beatrice, one for Benedick. Consider what type of people they are. Note down key headings such as choice of language, wit and humour, independence of spirit, and views on marriage. Develop your ideas and support them with brief references. Compare your ideas with a performance or adaptation.

Activity 2: Stagecraft

In a group, plan the production of a performance/adaptation of *Much Ado About Nothing*. Give each member of the group a non-acting role in the production, such as being responsible for production, costume and make-up, props, lighting, sound, or set design. Decide on the most important decisions or tasks that each member has to undertake, and make notes on each.

Activity 3: Theme

As you study *Much Ado About Nothing* decide on **two** important themes (e.g. love and deception), and note down moments in the play that deal with these. Give brief references from the text that support them.

Activity 4: Relationships

While working through the play, choose a relationship, e.g. Claudio and Hero. Think about how they relate to other characters in the play.

Draw up a page with two columns, one for the relationship and one for the textual evidence. In the first column note down headings for your ideas about the relationship. In the second column write down references from the text, using key words and phrases.

SAMPLE CONTROLLED ASSESSMENT TASK

> • Choose one important relationship in the Shakespeare drama text you have studied. Compare your reading of the relationship with the presentation of the same relationship in an adaptation.
> • Use examples from the text in your response.

Here are extracts from essays by two candidates who had each watched Kenneth Branagh's production of *Much Ado About Nothing* (1993) and compared this with their own reading of the play.

Extract 1 – Grade C response

Clear introduction

The play Much Ado about Nothing has many interesting characters, especially Beatrice and Benedick. Their relationship provides much of the humour in the original play, and in Branagh's production. Shakespeare's text emphasises the fact that neither Beatrice or Benedick wish to marry, with Beatrice saying 'I had rather hear my dog bark at a crow than a man swear he loves me.' These two insult each other as a way of hiding their real feelings. As the play progresses, the audience begin to see this, with Beatrice saying as if to Benedick: 'taming my wild heart to thy loving hand'.

Shows understanding of relationship

Apt quotation, but needs more comment

Branagh's version also places emphasis on the relationship between Beatrice and Benedick and their first quarrel is one of the best scenes. It is easy for the audience to see the sparks of love underneath the insults Shakespeare wrote. It makes it more believable when at the end Beatrice has written, according to Hero ('writ in my cousin's hand'), a love poem (a sonnet) to show how she feels about Benedick. At the time the film was released, also, it had to compete with many modern romantic comedies. The lively relationship between Beatrice and Benedick is like many relationships you see in those films. In this way, you can see that Shakespeare managed to create a type of relationship between these characters that is still popular nowadays.

A personal response to the film

A valid point, but more detail needed

Reference needs to be more specific

Examiner's comments

- This extract shows a sound overall understanding of the relationship with some useful quotations.
- For a higher grade, the examples of language could have been analysed more fully to show how Shakespeare explores the developing feelings.
- The personal response to what makes the characters' attitudes interesting in the film could have been supported with closer reference.
- As it stands, this is a Grade C response.

Extract 2 – Grade A response

Shakespeare's presentation of love in Much Ado about Nothing centres on two couples. However, Beatrice and Benedick catch the attention of the reader most, rather than Claudio and Hero. The relationship between Benedick and Beatrice seems even livelier, and more entertaining than the open declarations of love made by Hero and Claudio ('That I love her, I feel'). Benedick is a witty misogynist referring to women's sharp tongues and that they are sometimes inclined to be fickle sexually. However, the play turns traditional fears of women's inconstancy upside down, especially when Balthasar sings 'sigh no more, ladies...men were deceivers ever'. Thus, Beatrice is constant in her love to Benedick, and her sharp tongue is merely a fitting foil for Benedick's wit.

Kenneth Branagh directed and starred as Benedick in the 1993 film adaptation of the play, which is mostly true to the text and to the original play's spirit. In Benedick's quarrels with Beatrice in the film, the use of physical comedy emphasises the text (pulling extraordinary faces to reveal his feelings, falling off a deckchair). The lines create laughter, but so does the way they are set up and delivered. Expressions and actions play a large part in the comedy and the poignancy of their relationship. These effects do not appear on the written page but, combined with the real-life chemistry of the two actors, they make it all the more believable when Beatrice states 'I love you with so much of my heart that none is left to protest.'

Margin annotations:
- Valid comment on the two couples
- Interesting comment on Benedick's attitudes to women
- Varied, effective vocabulary
- Ambitious and telling observation
- Good comparative point
- Strong point with perceptive explanation

Examiner's comments

- This is a perceptive assessment not only of the way the relationship is presented in the original text but also in the film.
- It makes excellent use of integrated quotations to support the analysis and shows an awareness of aspects of visual humour which added to the enjoyment in Branagh's production.
- Discriminating comparisons are explored.
- The style is fluent and terminology is used appropriately.
- This is a Grade A response.

How to succeed in WJEC English Literature

Much Ado About Nothing is one of the set drama texts for the Unit 2a (Literary heritage drama and contemporary prose) examination.

The exam question on *Much Ado About Nothing* will be in two parts. The first part will focus on an extract from the play, which is printed in the exam question paper. Your response will be worth 10 marks. The second part will consist of a choice of two essays. You will choose one question to answer and your response will be worth 20 marks.

You should spend about 20 minutes on your response to the printed extract, and about 40 minutes on the essay.

The extract question

The extract is always the same for both Higher and Foundation tiers. The questions are similar, but the Foundation question will be rather more straightforward, with more emphasis on 'what' rather than 'how', and will be more likely to remind you of the need to support your answer with words and phrases from the extract.

How to get a good grade

Before you start responding to the extract question, think carefully:

- Take note of the question and decide exactly what it is asking for (i.e. your interpretation of the extract) – this will form the basis of your response. Support your views with close reference to the text.
- Be prepared to put the extract in context. This could be a useful starting point for your response.
- As you read the extract, underline key words and phrases that support your interpretation. It's important to cover the whole of the extract, make sure you go right to the end. Try to select details from the beginning, the middle and the end, and then from key points in between.

As you start **writing** your response:

- Make sure you have a strong opening, making specific points at the start. For example, if the question asks you to discuss the mood and atmosphere in the extract, say what you think the mood and atmosphere is. Or, if the question asks you for your thoughts and feelings about a character, make your point of view immediately clear.
- As you make points, stay focussed by referring back to the question.
- For every point you make, prove it with evidence from the extract. Aim to keep the evidence brief. Long quotations don't earn you any more marks, and give you less time to discuss your points.
- Explain how your evidence or selected detail supports the point you have made. (Some people use the expression 'PEE', or **P**oint, **E**vidence, **E**xplanation, to remind them about this.)

Look closely at how Claudio and Don Pedro speak and behave in this extract. What impressions would an audience receive of their characters?

Extract: Act 1 Scene 1, lines 245 to 285 (pages 25–6)

From: My liege, your Highness now may do me good ...

To: ... In practice let us put it presently.

Here are extracts from essays by students.

Extract 1 – Grade C response

Clear context	In this extract, which takes place at the start of the play, just after the soldiers have returned from battle to Messina, Claudio asks Don Pedro for help and advice in gaining Hero's love. He asks about Leonato, Hero's father, and Don Pedro quickly guesses his motive, asking, 'Dost thou affect her, Claudio?'. Claudio explains that he couldn't do much about it before, when they were going to war,
Reference to text – could develop more	but now he has time to think about her in that way. Don Pedro offers to help him out by having a word with Leonato and Hero. Claudio seems to think it's a bit fast:

Awareness of character, with support

Simple comment on selected detail

'...lest my liking might too sudden seem,
I would have salved it with a longer treatise.'
He is saying here that it might seem too sudden.
But Don Pedro is confident that everything will be fine and takes charge.

Beginning to discuss characters and relationship

Examiner's comments

- There is clear awareness of what is going on here and some discussion of characters and relationships.
- Some of the points made are clearly explained, and supported by direct reference to the detail of the extract.
- Still more focus on individual words or phrases would also be worthwhile.
- As it stands, this is a Grade C response.

Extract 2 – Grade A response

Clear context

In this extract, from the beginning of the play, just after Don Pedro and his men have returned from war to the house of Leonato, the Governor of Messina, Claudio confesses to Don Pedro his attraction to Hero, Leonato's daughter. From Don Pedro's prompt response, it is clear that he is very keen on securing the match, and by the end of the extract, an audience would receive the impression that he is going to take over.

Good overview

Although Claudio tries to be subtle ('Hath Leonato any son, my lord?'), Don Pedro perceptively immediately guesses Claudio's motive for asking the question, 'Dost thou affect her, Claudio?'

Astute observation

Evaluative comment

There is an immediate contrast in the way the two men speak and behave, which quickly highlights the difference in power in their relationship. Claudio speaks rather tentatively:

'But now I am returned, and that war-thoughts
Have left their places vacant, in their rooms
Come thronging soft and delicate desires...'

while Don Pedro is more assertive, 'If thou dost love fair Hero, cherish it..'

Appreciation of tone – well supported

Examiner's comments

- This is a well-focused and perceptive start to a response.
- There is clear evidence of overview and evaluation.
- Points made are well supported by reference to the text.
- The student shows close reading and sensitive probing of the subtext.
- This is a Grade A response.

RESPONDING TO THE ESSAY QUESTION

For the longer, essay-style response, you will have a choice of questions. It is important to choose the one you feel you can do best. There is usually at least one question on a character or characters, and other types of questions may focus on themes, the title of the play, or on a particular part of the play (for example, why it is important to the play as a whole.)

As you write your essay, make sure you:

- have a good strong start, with clear reference to the question
- keep focused on the question throughout (a reference to it in every paragraph is a good idea)
- show the examiner you know the play in detail, but don't worry about long quotations – the shorter and more direct the reference the better
- select key parts of the play (and make sure you refer to the whole play, including its ending)
- have a clear and specific conclusion, summing up your main ideas.

Usually, the questions for Higher and Foundation tiers will be on similar topics. The difference between the tiers is that those on the Foundation tier are more likely to have bullet points to help you organise your answer, and/or to be worded in a straightforward way. To get a good mark on the Foundation tier, it is important to use all the bullet points to help you frame your answer. Higher tier questions will have more focus on 'how', and are less likely to have bullet points. On both tiers, you must be sure to show your knowledge of the **whole** play.

A typical Higher tier question might be:

> Look closely at how Claudio and Don Pedro speak and behave here.
> What impressions would an audience receive of their characters?

A typical Foundation tier question might be:

> What do you think of the way Claudio and Don Pedro speak and behave here? Give reasons for what you say, and remember to support your answer with words and phrases from the extract.

SAMPLE HIGHER TIER EXAMINATION QUESTION AND RESPONSES

> Show how Shakespeare presents the development of the relationship between Beatrice and Benedick.

Extract 1 – Grade C response

Context and focus

At the beginning of the play, Beatrice is with her uncle Leonato and her cousin Hero. She is asking about Benedick. She is making fun of the way he used to go on about how he would never fall in love, and how he goes on about fighting all the time. Everyone says good things about him, such as he has been brave in the wars and is 'pleasant' and 'a good soldier' but Beatrice says she thinks he is 'a stuffed man.' This may suggest that he is like a tailor's dummy, and therefore may look nice but is not a real man. However, I think that although Beatrice pretends not to be interested in Benedick, the fact that she keeps going on about him suggests she is really. Leonato says there is a 'merry war' between them. Beatrice asks lots of questions about Benedick. This again is a clue that she is actually keen on him, however much she is trying to pretend otherwise.

Discussion of selected detail

Personal response – reveals subtext

Astute inference – engaged discussion

When Benedick comes back with the other soldiers, he starts arguing with Beatrice nearly straight away. He calls her 'Lady Disdain'. They seem to play with words all the time such as when Beatrice responds, 'Courtesy itself must convert to disdain', and he replies, 'Then is courtesy a turncoat'. This suggests that although they seem to be arguing, they are in fact very similar, and well-suited. Benedick says he is 'loved of all the ladies' apart from Beatrice and she says, 'I had rather hear my dog bark at a crow than a man swear he loves me.' I think an audience would think they might get together because they have a love/hate relationship.

Supported discussion of characters and relationships

Reference to the text

Reference to the text

Personal, engaged response

Examiner's comments

- This opening to a response to the question has many positive qualities: it is engaged and shows a clear awareness of the relationship between the characters at this point in the play.
- There are relevant references to the text to support the points made.
- To move to a higher grade the student should discuss more thoroughly and thoughtfully the ways the characters speak and behave and could also look more closely at the impact of specific words and phrases.
- As it stands, this is a Grade C response.

Extract 2 – Grade A response

Throughout the play, Beatrice and Benedick engage in witty banter, while Shakespeare makes it clear to the audience how well-suited they are. Nevertheless, it is only at the very end that they finally admit their love for one another, after the intervention of their friends, who are also convinced of the suitability of the match. Even then, they still maintain their verbal sparring, as Benedick claims 'I take thee for pity', whilst Beatrice counters this by saying she will 'yield....partly to save your life.'

> **Clear focus and overview**

> **Well-selected detail**

Although they have known each other some time, at the start of the play Benedick has been away at war, and the way in which Beatrice enquires after him, whilst she may appear to be hostile to him (the messenger notes, 'I see, lady, the gentleman is not in your books') may indicate that she is more interested in him than she is prepared to admit, even to herself. In their first exchange, they immediately take up where, presumably, they left off, each giving as good as they get. The repartee is so quick that it is hard for anyone else to keep up with it:

> **Context**

> **Apt reference**

> **Astute – sensitive to character**

BENEDICK Well, you are a rare parrot-teacher.

BEATRICE A bird of my tongue is better than a beast of yours.

The way these lines bounce off one another highlights the compatibility of Beatrice and Benedick, although at this point in the play, both vehemently deny any interest in the opposite sex, as Benedick declares 'I love none', to which Beatrice counters, 'I had rather hear my dog bark than a man swear he loves me.'

> **Style and effect**

> **Sensitive to characters and relationship**

Examiner's comments

- There is a clear overview of the relationship and evaluation of how the characters speak and behave.
- The technique of starting with reference to the ending of the play makes the overview particularly evident.
- Direct reference to the text is well handled, in the form of aptly chosen, concise quotations, and there is clear appreciation of the effects of the way the characters speak and behave.
- This is a Grade A/A* response.